Amos C. Hubbard

with respects of S. H. L.

MEMORIAL.

Eng^d by S. A. Schoff

DANIEL WEBSTER.

Danl Webster

A

MEMORIAL

OF

DANIEL WEBSTER,

FROM

THE CITY OF BOSTON.

BOSTON:
LITTLE, BROWN AND COMPANY.
1853.

RIVERSIDE, CAMBRIDGE:
PRINTED BY H. O. HOUGHTON AND COMPANY.

STEREOTYPED BY STONE AND SMART.

PREFACE.

The death of Mr. Webster, mourned throughout the whole country as a great national loss, fell with peculiar weight upon the community among whom he had so long lived; and the expressions of feeling which followed were proportionately numerous and emphatic. The object of the present volume is to gather up and preserve, in a permanent form, the various testimonials of respect to his memory which were called forth in Boston, whether by the City Government, or the various Associations of the citizens themselves. It was supposed that such a collection would be valued and cherished by the people of Boston and its vicinity, and not without interest to the community generally. The task of the editor has been little more than that of selection and arrangement. The account of the illness and death of Mr. Webster was drawn up by Mr. Ticknor, from notes and memoranda taken at Marshfield at the time.

G. S. H.

BOSTON, December, 1852.

CONTENTS.

PAGE

Mr. Webster's Last Autumn at Marshfield 1

Illness and Death 13

Proceedings of the City Council.

Proceedings in the Board of Mayor and Aldermen . . 29

Proceedings in the Common Council 33

Proceedings in the Court of Common Pleas 39

Meeting at Faneuil Hall 45

Proceedings of the Circuit Court of the United States for the District of Massachusetts . . . 73

Proceedings in the Supreme Judicial Court of Massachusetts 123

Proceedings of the Boston School Committee . . . 137

Proceedings and Resolutions of various Associations.

Proceedings of the Webster Executive Committee. . . 159

Proceedings of the Whig Ward and County Convention 161

Proceedings of Granite Club, No. 1 163

Proceedings of the Webster Under-Voters 167

Meeting of the Boston Merchants 169

Proceedings of the Board of Brokers 171

Proceedings of the Mercantile Library Association . . 173

Proceedings of the Mechanic Apprentices Library Association 175
Proceedings of Massachusetts Society of the Cincinnati 177
Orders of the Governor of Massachusetts 181
Proceedings of the Bunker Hill Monument Association 183
Proceedings of the Massachusetts Charitable Mechanics' Association 185
Proceedings of the Boston Marine Society 187
Proceedings of the Sons of New Hampshire 189
Proceedings of the President and Fellows of Harvard College 191
Proceedings of the Massachusetts Historical Society . . 193
Proceedings of the American Academy of Arts and Sciences 195

FUNERAL 201

PROCESSION AND SERVICES ON THE THIRTIETH OF NOVEMBER 217

EULOGY 231

MR. WEBSTER'S

LAST AUTUMN AT MARSHFIELD.

The following article, written by Professor Felton, appeared in the *Boston Courier* of October 20. It was prompted by a presentiment in the mind of the writer that the illness, under which Mr. Webster had been long laboring, must terminate fatally, and by a wish to prepare the public for the great loss that was so soon to fall upon them. On this account, as well as from its appropriate tone of thought and feeling, it is here republished.

MR. WEBSTER'S

LAST AUTUMN AT MARSHFIELD.

THE illness, under which Mr. Webster has suffered at Marshfield, has excited serious alarm. The loss of this eminent and illustrious statesman at the present moment would not only be a heavy calamity to the great interests of the country, but would strike the national heart with unspeakable sorrow. At his age, the disease, which has greatly impaired his physical strength, could but excite sad forebodings of the result. At all events, the day cannot be far distant when that comprehensive wisdom and consummate genius will be taken away from us, in the ordinary course of the life of man. There is now, however, reason to think that repose, and the invigorating breath of sea and land at Marshfield, will restore the health of the great Secretary, and send him, in due time, back to his post in Washington, to close the important questions still pending between our government and foreign countries. A few weeks longer, passed in the midst of the beloved scenes to which Mr. Webster has for so many years delighted to withdraw from the cares of public and professional life, will, it is earnestly hoped, carry him safely through this annual attack, and strengthen his heart for another winter of strenuous toil in the service of his country. We can ill spare Mr. Webster at any time ; but, at the present hour, his luminous intellect and commanding statesmanship, and his influence, potent for his country's good throughout the world, are needed in no common measure. Let us pray God that his life may still be spared, to meet and overcome the pressing urgency of our foreign affairs, and to shed upon us the light of his calm wisdom for many years to come. Whether in office or out of office, the knowledge that Mr. Webster is still among us strengthens our confidence that all will be well with the country. We know that we can still trust in the powers of an intellect that never fell below the requirements of the most critical occasion, and a patriotism that never shrunk from any labor or any sacrifice, which the supreme good of the country demanded. We have seen him defend the Constitution, with logic and eloquence never equalled in parliamentary history, when the admiration and applause of the world rewarded the great achievement. But this is not the hardest task to perform, nor the highest claim to a nation's gratitude. It is a nobler duty of patriotism to save the country from itself; to protect it from the excess of excited feelings, and passions overwrought; to step in between contending frenzies, and arrest their heady course before they grapple in a struggle to the death; to expose one's self to heavy blows on either side ; to fall, it may be, between the exasperated parties, and, at the risk of temporarily losing every object of personal desire, to rescue the commonweal. And this lofty duty of patriotism becomes severer when the excesses of cherished sentiments of philanthropy are to be rebuked, and the resentments of warm-hearted, philanthropic men and parties are to be encountered in checking their headlong race, before the safety of the country is fatally imperilled. The leading passion of our age, and of this part of the country, is enthusiastic devotion to the idea of the universal rights and the brotherhood of man. We are not content to bide the slow course of time; but rush, with fierce philanthropy, to the overthrow of institutions inconsistent with these ideas, — running every hazard, and trampling down every obstacle, however deeply rooted, that lies in the way of the immediate accomplishment of our generous desires. We despise the wisdom of the parable of the Tares and the Wheat; we insist on plucking out the one, even at the risk of destroying the other. We chafe impatiently at the restraints which the Constitution lays upon us, and which seem to forbid our eager aspirations to right a theoretic wrong. We struggle against its requirements, and seek, in fine-spun reasoning, the pretext on which we may break the guaranties our fathers undoubtedly meant in good faith to establish. This has been the tendency of the abolition and the anti-slavery movement at the North. The danger that sentiments, in themselves just and flowing from deep sources in the human heart, may overstep the bounds of constitutional action, has long been a cause of anxiety among men, on whom the burden of sustaining the government of the country rests. The influence of Mr. Webster's genius carries with it a heavy responsibility, as to the direction in which that influence shall be exerted. Ordinary men may ride their hobbies, and the world look on with indifference; they may declaim commonplaces of sentimental philanthropy, with all the comfort of knowing that the course of events will not be in the least affected thereby; they gain with their partisans all the honors of devotion to a great cause, with no fear of hazardous consequences resulting from the utterance of extreme or fanatical opinions.

But this cheap philanthropy of phrases and rhetorical commonplace is an indulgence which men, placed by intellect or position at the head of affairs, cannot safely indulge in. The strong tendency of generous sentiment, when not restrained by prudence, to override the prescriptive rights secured by constitutions and compacts, the great statesman and guide of men must sternly resist, even if resistance expose him to slander and vituperation, to the distrust of former friends, to the misunderstanding of his motives, to the charge of being a traitor to principles which his whole life has pledged him to uphold. Such crises, requiring the highest order of statesmanship and a moral courage that shrinks from no personal sacrifice for the general good, — periods when *reipublicæ salus est suprema lex,* — arise in the history of every great nation; and woe to that nation which has not the men of civic virtue equal to the peril of the time. This test of greatness and statesmanship Mr. Webster has nobly dared to stand; and he has reaped the consequences of calumny and vehement attack, made with an unscrupulous disregard of truth, a ruthless contempt of the decencies of controversy, in proportion to the greatness of the service, and the ardor of the philanthropic passions whose mad career he has helped to arrest. The violence of the storm is passed; the weight of character and intelligence in the country is on his side; the verdict of approval has been pronounced by a vast majority of the calm and clear-headed citizens of the United States. Thousands, who thought him wrong at first, now see that he was right, and heartily acknowledge the debt of gratitude they owe to his firmness and sagacious forecast. The union of the States, having been on both sides rudely assailed, is again consolidated. Hostile and incongruous fanaticisms may beset the CONSERVATOR on this side and on that. He has measured their force, breasted their onset, and foiled their purposes of mischief. Both great parties of the country have vindicated his wisdom, by acquiescing in the patriotic course marked out by his far-seeing policy, for the settlement of the most dangerous question that ever menaced the welfare of the nation. A vindictive philanthropy, here and there and from time to time, reopens the floodgates of slander, in the vain hope of disturbing the great statesman's repose. The firm earth does not stand with more unshaken solidity against the raving sea, as it roars and beats upon his Marshfield beach, than he stands unmoved in the magnanimity of his character, and the upholding power of conscious rectitude, looking down upon the ignominious efforts of foiled enemies to undermine the grandeur of his position.

"The Farm" at Marshfield is worthy to be the resting-place of its illustrious owner. It is shielded, by a range of beautiful hills, from the violence of our north-easterly storms. It has a distant view of the ocean, beyond the lowlands, which every high tide overflows. On one side, a wooded promontory juts into the sea; and on the other rises a sloping highland, on the brow of which, in the deep repose of nature, his kindred rest in their long sleep, with no sounds above or around them but the murmurs of the wind through the foliage of the drooping trees, or the song of birds, or the solemn voice of the sea, speaking eternally from its vast depths. The undulating surface sweeps up from the marshes and forms a tableland, on which the house is built; then gently falls into a smooth and spreading lawn; then, by a steeper slope, it ascends to the western range of hills, which, on that side, shut in the picture, and bound a scene of harmonious, yet richly varied and sweetly contrasted beauty. As you look down from these hills, your heart beats with the unspeakable emotion that such objects inspire; but the charm is heightened by the reflection, that the capabilities of nature have been unfolded by the skill and taste of one whose fame fills the world; that an illustrious existence has here blended its activity with the processes of the genial earth, and breathed its power into the breath of heaven, and drawn its inspiration from the air, the sea, and the sky, around and above; and that here, at this moment, the same illustrious existence is, for a time, struggling in a doubtful contest with a foe, to whom all men must, sooner or later, lay down their arms. Here, but a few weeks since, Mr. Webster was accustomed to drive the transient guest over his estate;

visiting his fields, his ocean shore, his flocks, and his herds; pointing out the prospect, and speaking with tender emotion of the sad and happy memories the varied views recalled; conversing with the rustic neighbors whom he chanced to meet in kind and genial tones, and on subjects which he and they understood alike; uttering, from time to time, glorious thoughts, suggested by the scene, in language of massive beauty and grandeur, which made the moment memorable in the listener's life. But this has been in some measure interrupted. That noble form, that surpassing strength of constitution, have drooped under the protracted illness which has withheld him from the turmoil raging outside of that secluded spot; the drives over the hills, and along the loud-resounding sea, which he loved so much, have ceased. Solemn thoughts exclude from his mind the inferior topics of the fleeting hour; and the great and awful themes of the future, now seemingly opening before him, — themes to which his mind has always and instinctively turned its profoundest meditations, — now fill the hours won from the weary lassitude of illness, or from the public duties, which sickness and retirement cannot make him forget or neglect. The eloquent speculations of Cicero on the immortality of the soul, and the admirable arguments against the Epicurean philosophy, put into the mouth of one of the colloquists, in the book on the Nature of the Gods, share his thoughts with the sure testimony of the Word of God. But no day passes that the affairs of the country do not occupy his attention. His great mind never applied itself with a calmer or more comprehensive grasp to the duties of his department. The intellectual power asserts its supremacy over physical weakness and tedious disease, with an unfaltering energy of soul that in itself is a stronger argument of its immortality than Cicero ever uttered in the majestic accents of the Latin tongue.

These are the dignified pursuits that grace the days of suffering passed by the illustrious statesman of Marshfield. The respectful sympathies of the country surround him in his hours of illness, and the prayers of good men go up to Heaven for his speedy restoration. If it is written in the inscrutable decrees of God that he is to be recalled from the scene of his earthly labors before his work is completed, — if so heavy a bereavement is soon to fall on the American people,— may no man have cause to reproach himself that he strove to embitter the last moments of so illustrious a life by harsh imputations or slanderous speech. When Mr. Webster is withdrawn from the scenes of this world, the party asperities which have raged so fiercely round him will be drowned in the tears of a nation's grief; and he who has so far forgotten the claims of patriotic greatness as to join in the ignoble work of calumniating a long life, exhausted in memorable services to the country and the age, will bear in his heart the burden of an upbraiding conscience, and a sense of wrong done to the common benefactor of every American citizen, long after the day of atonement is passed. For, whatever heated partisans may say while Mr. Webster lives, hereafter, when the historian shall look back upon the first century of the American Republic, the two names which will shine with most unfading lustre and the serenest glory, high above all others, are Washington and Webster. There are men who are remembered only as the revilers of Washington; there may be men who will be remembered only as the slanderers of Webster.

ILLNESS AND DEATH.

ILLNESS AND DEATH.

Mr. Webster died at Marshfield, on Sunday morning, October 24th, 1852.

His health, as has been intimated in the preceding paper, had failed during the summer from his severe public labors and from the progress of an obscure disease in the liver of long standing, accelerated, no doubt, by the shock which his whole system had received when he was thrown from his carriage in the preceding May. He was aware of his decline, and watched it with a careful observation; frequently giving intimations to those nearest to him of the failure in strength which he noticed, and of the result which he apprehended must be approaching. Towards the end of September he seemed, indeed, to rally a little; but it was soon apparent to others, no less than to himself, that, as the days passed on, each brought with it some slight proof of a gradual decay in his bodily powers and resources.

On Sunday evening, October 10, he desired a friend, who was sitting with him, to read to him the passage in the ninth chapter of St. Mark's Gospel, where the man brings his child to Jesus to be cured, and the Saviour tells him, "If thou canst believe, all things are possible to him that believeth; and straightway the father of the child cried out, with tears, Lord, I believe, help thou mine unbelief." "Now," he continued, "turn to the tenth chapter of St. John, and read from the verse where it is said, 'Many of the Jews believed on him.'" After this he dictated a few lines, and directed them to be signed with his name and dated, Sunday Evening, October 10, 1852. "This," he then added, "is the inscription to be placed on my monument." A few days later, — on the 15th, — he recurred to the same subject, and revised and corrected with his own hand what he had earlier dictated, so as to make the whole read as follows: —

"Lord, I believe; help thou
mine unbelief."

Philosophical
argument, especially
that drawn from the vastness of
the Universe, in comparison with the
apparent insignificance of this globe, has sometimes shaken my reason for the faith which is in me;
but my heart has always assured and reassured me, that the
Gospel of Jesus Christ must be a Divine Reality. The
Sermon on the Mount cannot be a merely human
production. This belief enters into the
very depth of my conscience.
The whole history of man
proves it.

DANIEL WEBSTER.

When he first dictated this inscription, he said to the friend who wrote it down—"If I get well, and write a book on Christianity, about which we have talked, we can attend more fully to this matter. But, if I should be taken away suddenly, I do not wish to leave any duty of this kind unperformed. I want to leave somewhere a declaration of my belief in Christianity. I do not wish to go into any doctrinal distinctions in regard to the person of Jesus, but I wish to express my belief in his divine mission;"—solemn and remarkable words, by which it is plain that, having given the deliberate testimony of his life to the truth of Christianity, as a miraculous revelation of God's will to man, he desired, though dead, still to bear the same testimony from his grave to the same great truth. The monument on which he intended this striking inscription should be placed, he has elsewhere directed should be of "exactly the same size and form" with the modest monuments he had already erected, within the same inclosure, for his children and for their mother.

On Tuesday, the 19th of October, he was too feeble to appear at the dinner-table, and desired that his son might take his place at its head, till he should be able again to go down stairs; "or," he added, "until I give it up to him altogether." That evening was the last time his friends had the happiness to see him in his accustomed seat at his own hospitable fireside.

Warned by his increasing debility he had already given some directions concerning a final disposition of his worldly affairs; but he now desired that his will might be immediately drawn up in legal form, and the next day he dictated a considerable portion of it with great precision and a beautiful appropriateness of phraseology. Some of its directions are very striking, not only from their import, but from the simplicity with which their meaning is set forth: —

"I wish to be buried," he says, "without the least show or ostentation, but in a manner respectful to my neighbors, whose kindness has contributed so much to the happiness of me and mine, and for whose prosperity I offer sincere prayers to God."

After this, every thing relating to his personal concerns is wisely and well provided for, and all his immediate kindred tenderly remembered. He then goes on: —

"My servant, William Johnson, is a free man. I bought his freedom not long ago for six hundred dollars. No demand is to be made upon him for any portion of this sum; but, so long as is agreeable, I hope he will remain with the family. Monicha McCarty, Sarah Smith, and Ann Bean, colored persons, now also, and, for a long time, in my service, are all free. They are very well-deserving, and whoever comes after me, must be kind to them."

And then, with the usual legal forms, this remarkable and characteristic document is closed.

The day when the preparation of the will was completed — Thursday — was one in which Mr. Webster had attended to much public business, besides giving his usual careful directions about every thing touching his household and his large estate. It was intended, therefore, to postpone the final signing and execution of that paper until the next morning; more especially as his forenoons were uniformly more comfortable than the later portions of the day. But, in the afternoon, his complaint assumed a new and more formidable character. Blood was suddenly ejected from his stomach. The symptom was decisive. He fixed an intensely scrutinizing look upon Dr. Jeffries, — his attending physician and personal friend, — and inquired what it was? He was answered that it came from the diseased part. "What *is* it?" he repeated with the same piercing look, and then, without waiting for a reply, added, "*That* is the enemy; — if you can conquer *that*" — he was interrupted by a recurrence of the attack, but his mind, it was obvious, was already made up. He knew that his time must be short, and that whatever he had to do must be done quickly.

He determined, therefore, at once to execute his will. It was made ready and brought to him. He ascertained that its provisions and arrangements were entirely satisfactory to the persons most interested in them, and then, having signed it with a larger boldness and freedom in the signature than was common to him, he folded his hands together, and said solemnly, "I thank God for strength to perform a sensible act." In a full voice, and with a most reverential manner, he went on and prayed aloud for some minutes, ending with the Lord's Prayer, and the ascription, "And now unto God the Father, Son, and Holy Ghost, be praise forever more. Peace on earth, and good will towards men;" — after which, clasping his hands together, as at first, he added, with great emphasis, — "*That* is the happiness — the essence — *Good will towards men.*"

Much exhausted with the effort, he desired all but Dr. Jeffries and a favorite colored nurse, who had long been in his service, to leave the room, that he might rest. But, before he slept, he said, "Doctor, you look sober. You think I shall not be here in the morning. But I shall. I shall greet the morning light."

The next forenoon, he repeated a similar assurance to his kind and faithful physician, who, as he thought, again looked sad, though he was only overcome with fatigue and long watching. "Cheer up, Doctor — cheer up — I shall not die to-day. You will get me along *to-day.*" And so he went on through Friday, giving comfort and kind thoughts to all who surrounded him. In the course of the morning, he attended to the public business that needed immediate care, and gave directions for every thing about his farm and household as usual, and, in the evening sent for the person who managed his affairs, and directed him, with more than his customary exactness, concerning all arrangements for the next day.

But when the next day — Saturday — came, he felt as he had not felt before. He felt that it was his *last* day. About eight o'clock in the morning, therefore, he desired that all in the room should leave it, except Dr. Jeffries, who had been his physician for a long period, and who had now been in constant attendance on him, living in the house, for above a week. During the night Mr. Webster perceived that he had grown weaker by excessive loss of blood from the stomach. He had just suffered afresh in the same way. But when he was certain that he was alone with his professional adviser, and that no loving ear would be pained by what he should say, he spoke in a perfectly clear and even voice, but with much solemnity of manner, and said, "Doctor, you have carried me through the night. I think you will get me through the day. I shall die to-night." The faithful physician, much moved, said, after a pause, "You are right, Sir." Mr. Webster then went on:—"I wish you, therefore, to send an express to Boston for some younger person to be with you. *I shall die to-night.* You are exhausted, and must be relieved. Who shall it be?" Dr. Jeffries suggested a professional brother, Dr. J. Mason Warren, adding that he was the son of an old and faithful friend of Mr. Webster. Mr. Webster replied instantly, "Let him be sent for."

Dr. Jeffries left the room to prepare a note for the purpose, and, on returning, found that Mr. Webster had made all the arrangements necessary for its despatch, having given minute directions who should go;—what horse and what vehicle he should use;—what road he should follow;—where he should take a fresh relay;—and how he should execute his errand on reaching the city. He also desired that provision should be made for summoning some other professional friend, if Dr. Warren could not be found, or could not come; and, on being told that this, too, had been foreseen and cared for, he seemed much gratified, and said emphatically, "Right, right."

After some repose, he conversed with Mrs. Webster, with his son, and with two or three other of the persons nearest and dearest to him in life, in the most affectionate and tender manner, not concealing from them his view of the approach of death, but consoling them with religious thoughts and assurances, as if support were more needful for their hearts than for his own. On different occasions, in the course of the day, he prayed audibly. Oftener, he seemed to be in silent prayer and meditation. But, at all times, he was quickly attentive to whatever was doing or needed to be done. He gave detailed orders for the adjustment of whatever in his affairs required it, and superintended and arranged every thing for his own departure from life, as if it had been that of another person, for whom it was his duty to take the minutest care.

After nightfall, he received at his bedside each member of his family and household, the friends gathered under his roof, and the servants, most of whom having been long in his service had become to him as affectionate and faithful friends. It was a solemn and religious parting, in which, while all around him were overwhelmed with sorrow, he preserved his accustomed equanimity, speaking to each words of appropriate kindness and consolation which they will treasure hereafter among their most precious and life-long possessions.

During the whole course of his illness, Mr. Webster never spoke of his disease or of his sufferings, except in the most general terms, or in order to give information to his medical advisers; but it was plain to Dr. Jackson, who was twice called in consultation; to Dr. Warren, who was with him during the last night of his life; and to Dr. Jeffries, who was his constant attendant from the first, that he noted and understood every thing that related to his condition, and its successive changes. His conversation on this, as on all other subjects, was perfectly easy and simple; — the deep tones of his voice remained unchanged; — his gentleness was uniform; — and the expressions of his affection to those who approached him, and even to those who were absent, but who were carefully remembered by him in messages of kindness, were true, tender, and faithful to the end. No complaint escaped from him; nor did he show the least impatience under his infirmities, or the least reluctance to die. He felt the value and the power of life, and he was full of love for his home, and for all that surrounded him there and made him happy. But his submission to the will of God was entire. He said, on one occasion, "I shall lie here patiently until I die;" — and he did so. But, through those wearisome days, he preserved his natural manner in every thing, and maintained, without effort, those just and true relations between himself and all persons, things, and occurrences about him, which through life had marked him so strongly and had given such dignity and power to his character.

From the morning of Saturday, when he had announced to his attendant physician — what nobody, until that time, had intimated — that he "should die that night," the whole strength of his great faculties seemed to be directed to obtain for him a plain and clear perception of his onward passage to another world, and of his feelings and condition at the precise moment when he should be entering its confines. Once, being faint, he asked if he were not *then* dying? and on being answered that he was not, but that he was near to death, he replied simply, "Well;" as if the frank and exact reply were what he had desired to receive. A little later, when his kind physician repeated to him that striking text of Scripture,—"Yea, though I walk through the valley of the shadow of death, I will fear no evil, for thou art with me; thy rod and thy staff, they comfort me"—he seemed less satisfied, and said, "Yes;—but the *fact*, the *fact* I want;"—desiring to know if he were to regard these words as an intimation, that he was *already* within that dark valley. On another occasion, he inquired whether it were likely that he should again eject blood from his stomach before death, and, being told that it was improbable, he asked, "Then *what* shall you do?" Being answered that he would be supported by stimulants, and rendered as easy as possible by the opiates that had suited him so well, he inquired, at once, if the stimulant should not be given *immediately;* anxious again to know if the hand of death were not *already* upon him. And on being told, that it would not be *then* given, he replied, "*When* you give it to me, I shall know that I may drop off at once."

Being satisfied on this point, and that he should, therefore, have a final warning, he said a moment afterwards, "I *will*, then, put myself in a position to obtain a little repose." In this he was successful. He had intervals of rest to the last; but on rousing from them, he showed that he was still intensely anxious to preserve his consciousness, and to watch for the moment and act of his departure, so as to comprehend it. Awaking from one of these slumbers, late in the night, he asked distinctly if he were alive, and on being assured that he was, and that his family was collected around his bed, he said, in a perfectly natural tone, as if assenting to what had been told him, because he himself perceived that it was true, "I still live." These were his last coherent and intelligible words. At twenty-three minutes before three o'clock, without a struggle or a groan, all signs of life ceased to be visible; his vital organs giving way at last so slowly and gradually as to indicate,—what every thing during his illness had already shown,—that his intellectual and moral faculties still maintained an extraordinary mastery amidst the failing resources of his physical constitution.

And so there passed out of this world one of its great, beneficent, and controlling spirits. As the sun rose on that quiet Sabbath morning the expected, yet dreaded, event was announced as a public calamity, first, by the solemn discharge of minute guns, and afterwards by the tolling of bells, over a large part of the land — a spontaneous outbreak of the general feeling at the loss all had suffered. How heavily it fell on the hearts of men in this city, where he was best known, and especially what deep grief, mingled with bitter recollections of the past, and anxious forebodings for the future, marked each of the three memorable days,—consecrated as no three similar days ever were consecrated among us, to public mourning,—may be partly gathered from the records which this volume is intended to collect and preserve. The rest — little of which can be recorded — will dwell, among their saddest and most sacred thoughts, in the memories of all who shared in the moving services of those solemn occasions, or who gathered around that peaceful, sea-girt grave, and will be transmitted by them to their children, as the warning traditions of a great national sorrow.

PROCEEDINGS OF THE CITY COUNCIL.

PROCEEDINGS IN THE BOARD OF MAYOR AND ALDERMEN.

At an early hour of the morning of Monday, October 25, the Mayor issued an order for a special session of the Board, to testify their sense of the great loss which the City of Boston had sustained in the death of Mr. Webster; and to consult as to the measures proper to be adopted to honor his memory. On taking the chair, His Honor addressed the Board as follows:

Gentlemen of the Board of Aldermen, — I have called this special meeting of the Board to perform the painful duty of officially announcing to you the death of the Honorable Daniel Webster, Secretary of State of the United States. He died calmly and peacefully at his residence in Marshfield, yesterday (Sunday) morning, between the hours of two and three o'clock, and the country is overwhelmed with sorrow at this mournful event. There are seasons, Gentlemen, when the heart is too full for utterance, and this is eminently one of them. I shall not, therefore, attempt to obtrude, upon this solemn occasion, any poor words of my own, but leave to your good judgment to adopt such measures as may be befitting, to testify the deep sense entertained by the Board, and the citizens generally, of the great loss which has been sustained by this afflictive dispensation.

As early as practicable after the sad intelligence was received here, I caused the bells of the churches to be tolled, to announce the event to the people.

The Chair is now ready to receive any proposition that may be made.

Alderman OBER then addressed the Board as follows:

Mr. Mayor, — I rise in conformity with the promptings of my heart, to offer an order for the appointment of a committee to report such measures as shall be appropriate to testify the great respect and attachment we all of us feel for him whose loss we now lament — him whom we have ever regarded as the pillar of our constitutional liberty and as the friend of the oppressed in every nation — whose opinions and sentiments will ever shed upon his name a lustre which cannot be obliterated.

Whereas, His Honor the Mayor has announced to this Board the death of the Honorable Daniel Webster, Secretary of State of the United States; therefore,

Resolved, That this information is received by us with the most profound feelings of respect and veneration for the illustrious character of the deceased, and with the deepest grief for the loss which has been sustained by the cause of Humanity and true Constitutional Liberty throughout the world.

Resolved, That while in common with the whole American people we feel the death of Mr. Webster to be a great *National calamity,* we cannot but also feel, that to the inhabitants of this city of his early adoption, and with whom for nearly half a century his name and fame have been so closely identified, this national calamity is also a sad domestic bereavement.

Resolved, That the City Council, in a body, will attend the funeral of Mr. Webster at Marshfield; that the members thereof will wear crape on the left arm for the space of thirty days; and that the same badge of mourning for the illustrious deceased, and for the same length of time, be recommended to the citizens generally.

Resolved, That a joint special Committee be now appointed, to consider and report forthwith, what measures it is expedient for the City Council to adopt in further testimony of that profound respect and veneration for the memory of Mr. Webster, which the whole community so deeply feel and desire publicly to express.

Resolved, That the City Council, as the representatives of the people of Boston, tender to the family of Mr. Webster their most sincere and heartfelt sympathy in this season of their deep sorrow and affliction, and that a copy of these resolutions, under the seal of the City, be transmitted to Mrs. Webster, and also to the President of the United States.

Alderman Reed seconded the Resolutions, and, in doing so, addressed the Board as follows:

There seems to be little occasion for any remarks at the present time, from any member of this Board. The news of the death of Mr. Webster is now rapidly flying to the remotest extremities of the country, and the heart of this nation is at this moment filled with the same feelings and thoughts with which our own minds are occupied; and these may, perhaps, be as well expressed by silence as by words.

It seems to me to have been among the most fortunate events of the present municipal year, that Mr. Webster received the unanimous invitation of the City Council to address his fellow-citizens in Faneuil Hall, and that the invitation was accepted by him. We have reason to think that this occurrence was highly grateful to his own feelings, as it was honorable to the City Council and acceptable to the citizens.

The opportunity then afforded to the members of this Board, of presenting their respects to him formally, will always remain among their most cherished recollections; and the citizens, who were present at Faneuil Hall, will tell their children and their children's children, that they saw and heard Daniel Webster. Could we, at that time, have foreseen how soon he would leave us, what solemnity, what intensity of interest, would have been given to the occasion!

The death, as well as the birth, of distinguished individuals, forms an epoch in the history of nations and of the world; and I have sometimes thought that there was a tendency in the providential course of events, for great men to cluster together in their death as in their life. However this may be, the present year will be forever memorable in the annals of history, for the deaths of distinguished men, — men whose death caused a profound sensation not only throughout their own country, but throughout the world. I need only mention the names of Henry Clay, the Duke of Wellington, and Daniel Webster.

The Resolutions were here passed with great unanimity. The Mayor appointed Aldermen Ober, Reed, Rich, and Cary, a Committee on the part of the Board.

The Board then took a recess, to allow concurrent action of the Common Council.

PROCEEDINGS IN THE COMMON COUNCIL.

The lower branch of the City Council convened shortly after the hour of the upper branch, the President, Henry J. Gardner, Esq., in the chair.

On calling the Council to order, Mr. Gardner spoke as follows.

Gentlemen of the Common Council — This special meeting of the Council has been convened on a most solemn occasion. The letter I hold in my hand, from his Honor the Mayor, contains the official announcement that Daniel Webster is no more.

Seventy-one years ago next January, in a rude farm-house, then the most northerly inhabited by a white man in the interior of New England, Mr. Webster first saw the light, with no birthright but the good name of his father and the prayers of a pious mother. His early years were passed amid the wild beauties of the mountain district of New Hampshire, then clothed in their primeval forests; his physical powers developed by the labors of the farm on that stern soil, and his mental faculties quickened by the legends and traditions of his paternal hearth.

In due time, we find him transferred to the venerable Academy at Exeter, and thence to Dartmouth College. After his graduation, he taught school in the western part of Maine for a season, and then he entered, with his characteristic assiduity and ardor, on the study of his profession. During a few years we see him putting aside his hopes of fame and professional aspirations, to watch the declining health of his father, and to lighten or remove the home labors that weighed upon him. At that parent's decease, he removed to the then capital of his native State, — Portsmouth. Here acquiring fame, wider and wider extended every year, he at length was elected, once and again, a member of Congress.

It may be worthy of mention that, during his long public life, he was a candidate directly before the people but five times, and was never defeated. At his first election to Congress, from New Hampshire, and at his first, too, from Massachusetts, he led his ticket very largely; and on his reëlection, in both instances, and also on his election as a member of the Convention to revise our State Constitution, he had no organized opposition. So surely does the community pay homage to surpassing intellect, when accompanied and graced by purity of private life.

But it is not needful to trace him step by step farther. From his removal to our city, his name becomes historic, — his words and deeds and life are household themes. Henceforth the farmer's son, from an obscure section of New Hampshire, becomes the statesman, jurist, orator, patriot, — at whose words listening senates were convinced, whose mind swayed the destinies of mighty nations, and at whose death a whole country now mourns.

A great light is extinguished, and the world is the darker for it. We had three distinguished statesmen, differing in their intellectual tendencies, but towering amid and above the great men of our land; and now the last and the mightiest has left us.

Since most of us came upon the sphere of manhood, we have looked to him in his meridian splendor with love, and admiration, and devotion. We have listened to his words of power, have studied his comprehensive writings, and turned to him, not in vain, when doubt and darkness overshadowed the future.

But it is not we, — not a State, or section, or party, — whose loss alone is irreparable; our country weeps her ablest son; the Constitution, its exponent and defender; the Union, for which he perilled hopes and friends, esteem and love, — the Union mourns its warmest advocate.

It was but yesterday, as it were, that we, as a body, saw him and heard him; heard that eloquence which lives now but in memory, and, in a few short years, will be historic only. The words of the world's great poet apply to him —

> "That, when he speaks,
> The air, a chartered libertine, is still,
> And the mute wonder lurketh in men's ears
> To steal his . . . . . sentences."

But he is gone. The world has poured out its rich treasury of gifts upon him, "honors and fame and troops of friends," till there was nothing left to halo more greatness round the name of Daniel Webster.

And living thus honorably like a Christian patriot, he has died. How great the satisfaction that his undimmed mind, resigned and calm throughout, leaning on that faith we all should cling to, has passed cheerfully along the final road. He went calm, submissive, self-possessed—no duty unfulfilled—earth's greatest honors exhausted.

> "No cause for sorrow, then; but thankfulness,
> Life's business well performed,
> When weary age full willingly
> Resigns itself to sleep,
> In sure and certain hope.
> Oh end to be desired, whene'er as now,
> A life of service passed,
> The seasonable fruit of faith
> And good report,—and good
> Example have survived."

The President having concluded his remarks, read the following letter from the Mayor:

City Hall, Boston, October 25, 1852.

Henry J. Gardner, Esq., *President of the Common Council.*

Sir—I have summoned a special meeting of the members of the Common Council, for the purpose of communicating to them the proceedings of the Board of Mayor and Aldermen on the melancholy intelligence of the death of the Honorable Daniel Webster.

I respectfully ask your Board to take such measures as may be deemed proper, to testify their sense of the loss sustained by our city and the country, by this afflictive dispensation of Divine Providence. In order to announce the sad event, I caused the bells of the Churches to be tolled from 9 to 10 o'clock, yesterday morning.

Benjamin Seaver, *Mayor.*

The Resolutions were here unanimously passed in concurrence, the members of the Council rising, an event of unusual, if not unprecedented, occurrence. Messrs. Lawrence, Thompson, Haskell, Hale, Thomas, Calrow, and Nicholson, were joined to the Committee of the Board of Mayor and Aldermen. The Council then took a recess.

SECOND SESSION OF THE BOARD OF MAYOR AND ALDERMEN.

At the reassembling of the Mayor and Aldermen, the following Report was made by Alderman OBER:

The Joint Special Committee of the City Council, who were authorized, by an order of this date, to consider and report what further measures should be adopted to testify the loss this City and our Country has sustained, in the recent decease of the Honorable Daniel Webster; having attended to that duty, submit the following report.

First. That in addition to the measures suggested in the resolutions already adopted, the Committee recommend that the halls of both branches of the City Government, together with Faneuil Hall, be shrouded with emblems of mourning, such emblems to remain for the space of three months.

Second. That the American flag be immediately displayed at half-mast upon City Hall, on Faneuil Hall, and upon the flagstaff on the Common, and remain during the daytime every day, until after the funeral of Mr. Webster shall have taken place; and that merchants and masters of vessels in port be requested to display their flags at half-mast during the same time.

Third. That on the day set apart for the funeral, all public business be suspended; that the citizens be requested to close their places of business during the entire day; that signal guns be fired on the Common and on Blackstone Square every fifteen minutes, commencing at sunrise, and continuing until the hour fixed for the performance of the funeral ceremonies, when minute guns be fired for one hour, and during that hour all the bells in the city be tolled.

Fourth. That a eulogy on the life, character, and public services of Mr. Webster be pronounced before the government and citizens of Boston, in Faneuil Hall, by such individual, at such time, and attended by such ceremonies as the Committee hereinafter recommended to be appointed, shall determine.

Fifth. That a Committee, consisting of the Board of Mayor and Aldermen, the President of the Common Council, and one member of the Council from each ward, be appointed as a Committee of Arrangements, with full power to carry into effect the foregoing recommendations, and to take such other action in the premises as said Committee deem expedient and proper.

The report was unanimously accepted, and ordered to be sent down. Adjourned.

SECOND SESSION OF THE COUNCIL.

On the reassembling of the Council, a messenger was received from the other branch, bringing the above Report, offered by Alderman Ober. After remarks of a brief, pertinent, and eloquent character by Messrs. Hobart and Lawrence, the Report was unanimously adopted.

The President then appointed the following gentlemen on the Committee, on the part of this branch, mentioned in the last section of the above Report:

Messrs. Stearns, of Ward 1; Calrow, of Ward 2; Bradbury, of Ward 3; Lawrence, of Ward 4; Jewell, of Ward 5; Thomas, of Ward 6; Nicholson, of Ward 7; Haskell, of Ward 8; Thompson, of Ward 9; Lincoln, of Ward 10; Hale, of Ward 11; and Southard, of Ward 12.

The Council then adjourned.

PROCEEDINGS

IN

THE COURT OF COMMON PLEAS.

PROCEEDINGS IN THE COURT OF COMMON PLEAS.

At the opening of the Court of Common Pleas, on Monday morning, October 25, Hon. John C. Park, County Attorney, rose and spoke as follows:

May it please your Honor — I rise, with your permission, to make an announcement and offer a motion. I do this partly at the request of my friends of the Bar, and partly because it is my duty, holding the office, for the time being, of Attorney for the Commonwealth in these Courts, to notice an occasion, on which the Commonwealth, as such, has suffered an irreparable bereavement.

Daniel Webster, the Patriot, the Jurist, the Statesman, is no more.

I rise to pronounce no panegyric, no eulogy! This is neither the time nor occasion — nor am I the man. When the avalanche has fallen from the mountain top, when the thunderbolt has cleft the forest oak, deep silence succeeds the shock; and now the public pulse has ceased its throbbings, and holy, silent awe is the loudest oratory. Time will be, when we shall awake to a full realization of the event; and then eloquent lips will pour forth a nation's feelings.

How many thousands sympathize in the emotions of this hour! The news, lightning-winged, has already pervaded the Continent. The fisherman, on the Banks, pauses in his toil to echo back the wail, which reaches him from the shore. The trapper, in the valleys of the Rocky Mountains, catches it, as it rolls across the prairies. The industry of the nation feels that it has lost its best friend; — and even on the thrones of Europe, the monarchs of the Old World tremble as they learn that that master spirit, which has wielded a moral power over the destinies of nations more potent than their armed legions or their diplomatic machinery, now stands with Prophets of old and Apostles of truth, in humble adoration before the throne of Omnipotence.

Around us — in our very midst — how every thing speaks to us of him! Yonder monument to Liberty, baptized in the floods of his eloquence, yonder Pilgrim Rock, consecrated by his lips, in the spirit of Puritan truth, — the very landmarks and boundaries of our land, from the bleak Northeast to the sultry Southwest, are established under his wise, far-seeing guidance. Not a waterfall or cataract in all New England, rendered useful to mankind by those discreet measures which always met his cordial support, that did not seem on yesterday's holy morn, to have rolled its course seaward with a more subdued and plaintive murmur.

The Indian, when his Chief goes on his long pilgrimage to the spirit-land, buries with him his war implements, his tomahawk, and arrows. We, of a Christian faith, bury, *far away from* our Chief, the barbed arrows of political strife and party rancor, and gaze, with mournful gratitude, on the countless benefits which he has conferred upon us.

Threescore years and ten he has been spared to us. Thirty, at least, of the number, he has been leaving the impress of his gigantic intellect upon every prominent measure which has conduced to our country's advancement and prosperity.

But I forbear. The glorious sun has set. Unclouded to the last, its latent beams were of meridian splendor, and the twilight of good influences which it leaves will endure forever.

May it please your Honor — I feel sure that the Court will concur with the Bar, in believing that these halls of justice, from which we are to miss those eloquent tones, that impressive form, should, for a time be left to meditative silence. The old, who have met him in the arena of forensic warfare; the middle-aged, who have lost in him a kind friend and willing counsellor; the young, who have sat at his feet, and drank in lessons of deep wisdom from his lips; and even the young, struggling student, who, while he fully realizes the picture of the poet,

> "Haud facile emergunt quorum virtutibus obstat
> Res angusta domi,"

yet revived his drooping spirits with the remembrance of the perseverance and eventual success of the New Hampshire farmer's boy. All, all unite to mourn our loss.

I now move the Court, that this Court be adjourned for such interval as the proper discharge of our public duties may permit.

Judge PERKINS very briefly responded, remarking that, as it was understood further proceedings relating to Mr. Webster's death would take place in the Circuit Court to-morrow, he would add nothing to what had been said; and, in accordance with the wishes of the Bar, he would adjourn the Court to Thursday.

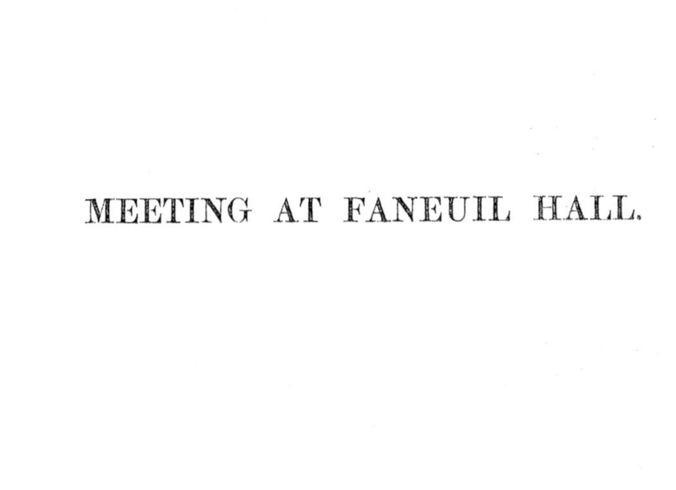

MEETING AT FANEUIL HALL.

MEETING IN FANEUIL HALL.

On the evening of Monday, October 25, a meeting of gentlemen was held at the Revere House, to consult together as to the measures proper to be adopted by the Citizens of Boston to show their respect to the memory of Mr. Webster, and their sense of the great loss sustained by them and the country at large in his death. After some discussion, the following call was drawn up, signed, and directed to be published in the papers of the next morning.

MEETING IN FANEUIL HALL.

All persons desirous to consult together and consider what memorial of the services of Daniel Webster is due to themselves and their country, are requested to assemble in Faneuil Hall to-morrow, (Wednesday) October 27th, at noon, for that purpose.

Edward Everett, William Hayden, George Ticknor, George S. Hillard, Joseph Tilden, Isaac Parker, Levi A. Dowley, T. B. Curtis, Samuel Hooper, John T. Heard, Benjamin Seaver, Samuel T. Dana.

Pursuant to the above call, the citizens of Boston assembled in Fanueil Hall, on Wednesday, October 27, at the hour of noon. Nothing could be more solemn and touching than the appearance of the Hall and the countenances of those who filled it. The windows had been darkened, and there was no light but that of the lamps. The citizens entered slowly and in silence, and conducted themselves as at the funeral of a friend; standing uncovered during the whole proceedings, and listening in profound stillness, broken only by sounds of audible grief. Not a single person ventured to disturb the sacred silence by any expression of applause; and even the "aye" of response returned to the resolutions was given faintly, and sounded like a moan. An occasion so solemn rarely comes within any one's experience; and the impression of that meeting will never be effaced from the hearts of those who were present.

The meeting was called to order by Hon. EDWARD EVERETT.

Messrs. William Hayden, Samuel Hooper, and Thomas Gray were appointed a Committee, to retire and report a list of permanent officers. The Committee subsequently reported, —

For President — His Honor Benjamin Seaver, Mayor of the City.

Vice-Presidents — Nathan Appleton, James Cheever, Robert G. Shaw, Charles Torrey, Charles G. Greene, Peter Harvey, Sidney Bartlett, Joseph Tilden, of Ward Six.

Secretaries — Samuel Kettell, J. Harris Smith, William W. Greenough, Samuel T. Dana.

The Report having been accepted, and the officers having taken their seats on the platform, Mayor SEAVER addressed the meeting as follows:

Fellow-citizens — I can do nothing more in the honorable position which, by your favor, has been assigned me, than to guide the proceedings of the meeting. The notice for the meeting explains every thing. Will the Secretary please to read it?

Mr. KETTELL accordingly read the call.

The MAYOR resumed his remarks, and said:

It is natural, on such a call as this, that the people of Boston should crowd this consecrated hall to indulge in the emotions of the heart, and mingle their sympathies on the afflictive event which has fallen so heavily upon our City, the State of Massachusetts, and the whole Country. It is good for us to be here. In contemplating the character of the illustrious man, whose death we mourn, we shall be made better men, better citizens, and be moved to the more faithful discharge of duty.

Daniel Webster was a constant and faithful friend of Boston, and of all her interests; they were dear to his heart; his labors and his life afford the most ample evidence of this. The people of our City, of the State, and of New England, are under the strongest obligations to him, and it is their duty to acknowledge them. There is not an individual here, be he rich or poor, of whatever profession, whom he has not directly or indirectly benefited. It is our duty to remember all this, and cherish a grateful sense of the benefits he has conferred upon us.

It is an interesting fact, which must be present to the minds of most of us to-day, that the last time he addressed the people of Boston in this Hall was on the 22d of May last, on the unanimous invitation of the City Government, *without distinction of party*. There are some circumstances attending this invitation worthy to be mentioned. It was my privilege to be a member of the Committee who visited Marshfield, to present the invitation. We found him suffering severely from the accident which occurred only a few days prior to our visit. The invitation was read to him, to which he listened with marked attention; and when he was told that it was given *without distinction of party*, his eyes filled with tears, and he said, with emotion, — "I shall accept the invitation, and will prepare an answer to be presented to the City Council." That eloquent and touching letter you all remember; and you also remember his equally eloquent and interesting address. He was too feeble in health, to make it prudent for him to leave his house; but so strong and ardent was his desire to meet his friends once more in Faneuil Hall, that he was willing to risk all for the gratification it afforded him. God be thanked that he had this opportunity!

But, fellow-citizens, we have not met here for the purpose of entering into any extended consideration of the character of our illustrious friend. This is not the time to do this.

The Chair is now ready to receive any proposition that may be made, to carry out the object of the meeting.

John T. Heard, Esq., then came forward, and said:

Mr. President — I ask permission to present resolutions expressive of the feelings of this community, occasioned by the death of an illustrious citizen. Daniel Webster, the orator, statesman, and patriot, he who counselled us in wisdom, is no longer amongst us. That voice, which we have so often heard echo through this hall, (Faneuil Hall,) in matchless eloquence, is silent; though its teachings of patriotism, and its advocacy of constitutional liberty and the rights of man, will speak forever. The whirlwind of political excitement and passion is hushed; and a solemn utterance of heartfelt sorrow is whispered from ear to ear. The resolutions will but faintly express the emotions of grief that pervade the breasts of the mourning multitude here assembled. I move, Mr. President, the following resolutions:

Whereas, It has pleased Divine Providence, to remove by death our late illustrious fellow citizen, Daniel Webster, we, the citizens of Boston, in Faneuil Hall assembled, desirous of giving utterance to those feelings of attachment and veneration which we cherish for his memory, unanimously adopt the following resolutions:

Resolved, That we are deeply sensible to the loss which has been sustained, not only by this community, but the State of Massachusetts and the whole Country, in the decease of a man, whose distinguished talents, learning, eloquence, and force of character, formed its brightest ornament; who, coming among us in early manhood, with a brilliant reputation from a sister State, rose by no slow ascent, till by the decease of his most eminent compeers, he stood, by all confession, the greatest of her great men; that, whether we contemplate in him the profoundly learned jurist, the advocate endowed with all the gifts of persuasion; the perfect master of the English tongue, in all the accomplishments of a scholar, a speaker, and a writer; the great interpreter and defender of the Constitution, whose luminous expositions of its revered text are replete with all the wisdom of the framers, and, who in moments of peril, rescued and sustained what they established; the model American Statesman, to whom the entire range of our political and Constitutional history, our diplomatic relations and foreign affairs, our great territorial, commercial, and industrial interests at home and abroad, were as familiar as household words; the enlightened patriot, to whom all parts of our common country, from North to South, and from ocean to ocean, were alike dear; who ever cherished with his whole heart that Union which makes us one people, and to the conservation of which his whole life was devoted; the philosopher and sage, whose volumes will furnish lessons of instruction, warning, and encouragement, to the latest posterity; the friend of constitutional freedom and liberty, protected by law, by whose burning eloquence, lending force to public opinion throughout the world, arbitrary power has been rebuked in its strong-holds, and nations struggling for their rights, have been cheered and strengthened; that, in fine, in whatever light we contemplate the great man whom we deplore, we want words to do full justice to our admiration of his mighty genius, our gratitude for his invaluable services, and our abiding sorrow over his grave.

Resolved, While in common with our fellow-citizens throughout the country, we lament the patriot and statesman, whose public labors and services have been of the utmost value to the country, that we, the inhabitants of Boston and of the Commonwealth of Massachusetts, the city and State of his adoption, mourn for the loss of a fellow-citizen, a neighbor, a companion, a friend, whose great heart was the dwelling of all the generous feelings; who delighted to unbend from the cares of state, and partake in the home-bred relaxations of private life; who, as a scientific and intelligent farmer, afforded to our substantial yeomanry a cheering example of successful practical husbandry; whose presence was the light and joy of every friendly circle; whose hospitable roof and genial fireside were the abode of all the domestic charities and kindly virtues of a true New England home; and who, having evinced through life, a reverence for the Bible and the ordinances of religion, found support in the last trying hour, in the hopes and promises of the Gospel.

And, whereas, we are desirous of testifying our respect for the memory of the departed, by some expression of our gratitude and veneration, which shall endure to other times, and convey to our children's children a lively impression of the feelings, which influence us. Be it further

Resolved, That an executive committee of one hundred persons be appointed by the Chair, to be selected in such manner as to represent the citizens of every pursuit, calling, and party, whose duty it shall be to take such measures as may be deemed expedient to provide, by the coöperation of the whole community, a permanent memorial of our illustrious and lamented fellow-citizen.

Resolved, That an attested copy of the foregoing resolutions be transmitted by the officers of this meeting, together with a report of its proceedings, to the bereaved family of Mr. Webster, with the assurance of the heartfelt and respectful sympathy of the citizens of Boston in their irreparable loss.

Hon. George S. Hillard moved the adoption of the resolutions, and said:

A great man has passed away from earth. A far-shining light is extinguished, and a strong column has fallen. We, who were guided by that light, who leaned upon that column, are left to walk by fainter rays, to rest upon feebler supports. I am not here to pronounce an eulogy upon Daniel Webster, nor you to hear one. A fresh grief is impatient of details. We are here to mourn, and not to praise him. You need not that I should unfold to you the treasures of his greatness. You need not that I should set forth to you his claims as a jurist, an orator, a statesman, and a patriot. You know them all too well. To suppose you ignorant of them, is to suppose you ignorant of the history of your country, where they are written in lines bright as the belt of Orion.

It is fitting for us to be here assembled, with these countenances of sadness. In the general bereavement, ours is a particular loss, for he belonged to us. It is now thirty years since he was sent by the citizens of Boston to take part in the councils of the nation, and since that time he has been the foremost man in this community. His eloquence has kindled, his wisdom has guided, his experience has taught us. All of us have turned, again and again, to look at his commanding presence, which, however often it might be seen, seemed an ever new expression of intellectual power and weight of character. Two generations of children have pointed him out to one another, as he moved along our streets. None of us, who have seen him, can ever have any other ideal image of greatness than that which his face and form have left upon our memories. He was our pride and our boast, whom we delighted to show to the stranger as the grandest growth of our soil and our institutions. "When the ear heard him, then it blessed him; and when the eye saw him, it gave witness to him."

But the influence which moved from here has gone forth to the ends of the earth. His voice of wisdom and power, which was at home among us, has penetrated wherever there was an oppressor to be rebuked, or a victim to be cheered. Everywhere it has brought hope to the struggling and the down-trodden, and confusion to the wrongdoer.

Not from one land alone, not in one tongue alone, will his death be mourned. From the four corners of the globe, tributes and testimony will be gathered up. The shepherd, who tends his flock beneath the clear skies of Greece; the cavalier, that spurs over the plains of South America; the Hungarian, pining in exile, or languishing in prison,—will all, when they hear of his death, feel a common grief at a common loss. Liberty will mourn a champion, humanity a friend.

There is a strong propriety in our meeting here, to do honor to the memory of this great man. With this spot his image is indissolubly associated. Here we have been accustomed to come together, to hang upon his words, to be guided by his counsels, and sustained by his strength. Here you have, again and again, looked upon his majestic form, and that noble, intellectual countenance, to which no artist has yet done full justice. Here you have seen him stretch forth that strong right hand of his, as if he were hollowing out for the mountain streams, the channels in which they should flow. Here you have heard his burning and powerful eloquence, — the lightning of passion running along the iron links of argument. Have seen, do I say? Have heard? Surely you see and hear him now. Evoked by the potent genius of the place, the departed hours and the departed man come back again. We need not that pictured canvas to recall his mighty presence. In the mind's eye, you see once more that heroic shape, that glowing and inspired countenance. In the mind's ear, you hear again that deeply-freighted voice, which has so often made the hearts of thousands swell and throb like one. The shadow of him we have lost, is more than the living forms of all who are left.

Great men are among the best gifts which God bestows upon a people. In this respect, He has not hidden his face from us. Great men have been among us, by whom we have been led and formed and upheld; men, wise in counsel, brave in action, earnest in patriotic purpose, and faithful to duty. Washington, Hamilton, Madison, Jay, Marshall, are illustrious names. History has none greater or better to show. And now another, — a commensurate spirit, — has been summoned away from the cares and trials of life, to take his place by their side. But we, that stand looking with weeping eyes into his open grave, should not forget to thank God for what we have had, for his threescore and ten years of rich and crowded life, for all that he has done for liberty and for law, for the confidence which his presence inspired, for the wisdom that saw the right, and the firmness that maintained it, for his great powers of thought and speech, for the precious legacy of his writings. Let us be thankful that such hands have shaped the moulds in which the opinions of so many have been cast.

It is now almost half a century since the nation was called upon to mourn the sudden and appalling death of the man who, by the greatness of his genius, and the greatness of his services, suggests the most obvious parallel to him who has just been taken from us. He died in the prime of his life, when his country had reason to expect many more years of valuable labor and influence. He died by what, if actions derive their character from the motives that prompt them, may be called a felon stroke and an assassin's hand. When the news of Hamilton's death smote upon the land, the general sorrow was mixed up with a burning sense of wrong, with a stupefying shock of surprise, and the wreck of high expectations suddenly dashed in pieces. Ours is a serener grief, for ours is a more natural, a more endurable bereavement. Daniel Webster had reached that period of life, when it becomes a man to set his house in order, and wait his final summons. As year after year passed by, and found us still leaning on his wisdom and experience, which the growth of the country and its widening relations made more and more important, when dates and the inexorable hours compelled us to admit that he was getting to be an old man, we could not help sometimes asking ourselves, to whom should we turn when this support should have been withdrawn? For some time past, though we have struggled against the conviction, we have been forced to acknowledge that time and toil were making inroads upon his vigorous frame. He has died full of years and full of honor, with no duty unperformed, and no trust undischarged. He has done his work and earned his crown. And as we have such cause for gratitude for his long and great life, so let us also be thankful for the mercy which so ordered its close; that he died by no lingering and painful decay, making him dead while yet living; that he died with all his glorious faculties unimpaired; and that this great orb, which had so long guided and cheered us with its light, sunk below the horizon, undimmed by a single cloud.

And there are other soothing and consoling reflections that temper this stroke. No man knoweth the place of his sepulchre. In the East, there is a touching benediction,—May you die among your kindred. This blessing was given unto him. He died as the heart hopes to die. He died in his own home, amid those scenes of natural beauty endeared to him by the joys and sorrows of many eventful years, with the faces of family, kindred, and friends, around his bed, religion pillowing his head, in that mellow and pensive season of the year so dear to his thoughtful and tender spirit, with his own trees waving before his dying eyes, and that voice of the sea, which he loved so well, soothing his dying ear:

> For him there is no longer any future,
> His life is bright; bright without spot it was,
> And cannot cease to be. No ominous hour
> Knocks at his door with tidings of mishap.
> Far off is he, above desire and fear;
> No more submitted to the chance and change
> Of the unsteady planets. Oh 'tis well
> With him! But who knows what the coming hour,
> Veiled in thick darkness, brings for us.

Yes, my friends, for us. These words are not inappropriate to the hour and the place. We are a great, a powerful, a prosperous people; but there are dangers in our path, and we know not what is hidden in the darkness of the coming hours. When we shall have discharged the last sad duty to this great statesman and patriot, and laid that illustrious head in the grave, who can fail to offer up a fervent supplication, that a double portion of his spirit may be upon us! May his influence help to save us from the evils of selfish ambition, of grasping injustice, of headlong fanaticism. May he continue to infuse into our councils the spirit of wisdom, the spirit of justice, and the spirit of peace.

What living man is so eloquent as death! What living lips can speak like those on which the grave has set its seal of silence! From the book of Job to the newspaper of to-day, the same teachings have been drawn from the dread presence, which no custom can make familiar. The cold and rigid frame, the mute tongue, the dim eye, the powerless hand, have ever given occasion to poets and moralists to discourse on the vanity of human wishes and the shadowy nature of human hopes. But the death of the great and good has other lessons than these. While it teaches impressively, that that which is mortal must die; it teaches also, not less impressively, that that which is immortal, shall not taste of death. "I still live," were among the last words of Webster. They are yet true. His works, his words, his examples, his life, still live. A death like his, so simply, so serenely great, — brightened by hope and faith and love, dignified with the perfect possession of such glorious powers, is not so much the close of one day as the dawn of another; not so much the putting off of mortality, as the putting on of immortality. When we read of such an euthanasia, we seem to hear a voice from the sky, which says, "Lift up that dejected brow, and the hands which are cast down. The death which you lament is but a great event in the life of the soul. It is a change, and not a dissolution. It is the gate to a new sphere, in which the mind, enriched with larger powers, shall enter upon broader fields of action and duty, where nobler struggles shall task the strength, and more precious crowns reward the victory; where the hopes and the dreams of earth shall be turned to sight, and the broken circles of life be rounded to the perfect orb."

Hon. EDWARD EVERETT then spoke as follows:

Mr. Mayor and Fellow-Citizens — I never rose to address an assembly when I was so little fit, body or mind, to perform the duty; and I never felt so keenly how inadequate are words to express such an emotion as manifestly pervades this meeting, in common with the whole country. There is but one voice that ever fell upon my ear which could do justice to such an occasion. That voice, alas! we shall hear no more forever. No more at the bar will it unfold the deepest mysteries of the law; no more will it speak conviction to admiring Senates; no more in this hall, the chosen theatre of his intellectual dominion, will it lift the soul as with the swell of the pealing organ, or stir the blood with the tones of a clarion, in the inmost chambers of the heart.

We are assembled, fellow-citizens, to pour out the fulness of our feelings; not in the vain attempt to do honor to the great man who is taken from us; most assuredly not with the presumptuous hope on my part to magnify his name and his praise. They are spread throughout the Union. From East to West, and from North to South, (which he knew, as he told you, only that he might embrace them in the arms of a loving patriotism,) a voice of lamentation has already gone forth, such as has not echoed through the land since the death of him who was first in war, first in peace, and first in the hearts of his countrymen.

You have listened, fellow-citizens, to the resolutions which have been submitted to you by Col. Heard. I thank him for offering them. It does honor to his heart, and to those with whom he acts in politics, and whom I have no doubt he well represents, that he has stepped forward so liberally on this occasion. The resolutions are emphatic, sir, but I feel that they do not say too much. No one will think they overstate the magnitude of our loss. Who that is capable of appreciating a character like that of Daniel Webster; who of us, fellow-citizens, that has known him — that has witnessed the masterly skill with which he would pour the full effulgence of his mind on some contested legal and constitutional principle, till what seemed hard and obscure became as plain as day; who that has seen him, in all the glory of intellectual ascendency,

> Ride on the whirlwind and direct the storm

of parliamentary conflict; who that has drank of the pure fountains of wisdom and thought in the volumes of his writings; who alas, sir, that has seen him

> in his happier hour
> Of social pleasure, ill-exchanged for power,

that has come within the benignant fascination of his smile, has felt the pressure of his hand, and tasted the sweets of his fireside eloquence, will think that the resolutions say too much?

No, fellow-citizens, we come together not to do honor to him, but to do justice to ourselves. We obey an impulse from within. Such a feeling cannot be pent up in solitude. We must meet, neighbor with neighbor, citizen with citizen, man with man, to sympathize with each other. If we did not, mute Nature would rebuke us. The granite hills of New

Hampshire, within whose shadow he drew his first breath, would cry shame; Plymouth Rock, which all but moved at his approach; the slumbering echoes of this hall, which rung so grandly with his voice; that "silent but majestic orator," which rose in no mean degree at his command on Bunker Hill — all, all would cry out at our degeneracy and ingratitude.

Mr. Chairman, I do not stand here to pronounce the eulogy of Mr. Webster; it is not necessary. Eulogy has already performed her first offices to his memory. As the mournful tidings have flashed through the country, the highest officers of Nation and State, the most dignified official bodies, the most prominent individuals, without distinction of party, the press of the country, the great voice of the land, all have spoken, and with one accord of opinion and feeling; and an unanimity that does honor at once to the object of this touching attestation, and to those who make it. The record of his life, from the humble roof beneath which he was born, (with no inheritance but poverty and an honored name,) up through the arduous paths of manhood, which he trod with lion heart and giant steps, till they conducted him to the helm of State — this stirring narrative, not unfamiliar before, has, with melancholy promptitude, within the last three days, been again sent abroad through the length and breadth of the land. It has spread from the Atlantic to the Mississippi. Struggling poverty has been cheered afresh; honest ambition has been kindled; patriotic resolve has been invigorated; while all have mourned. The poor boy at the village school has taken comfort as he has read that the time was when Daniel Webster, whose father told him he should go to college if he had to sell every acre of his farm to pay the expense, laid his head on the shoulder of that fond and discerning parent, and wept the thanks he could not speak. The pale student, who ekes out his scanty support by extra toil, has gathered comfort when reminded that the first Jurist, Statesman, and Orator of the time earned with his weary fingers by the midnight lamp the means of securing the same advantages of education to a beloved brother. Every true-hearted citizen throughout the Union has felt an honest pride, as he reperuses the narrative, in reflecting that he lives beneath a Constitution and a Government under which such a man has been formed and trained, and that he himself is compatriot with him. He does more, sir; he reflects with gratitude that in consequence of what that man has done, and written, and said — in the result of his efforts to strengthen the pillars of the Union — a safer inheritance of civil liberty, a stronger assurance that these blessings will endure, will descend to his children.

I know, Mr. Mayor, how presumptuous it would be to dwell on any personal causes of grief, in the presence of this august sorrow, which spreads its dark wings over the land. You will not, however, be offended if, by way of apology for putting myself forward on this occasion, I say that my relations with Mr. Webster run further back than those of almost any one in this community. They began the first year he came to live in Boston. When I was but ten or eleven years old, I attended a little private school in Short Street, (as it was then called, it is now the continuation of Kingston Street,) kept by the late Hon. Ezekiel Webster, the elder brother, to whom I have alluded, and a brother worthy of his kindred. Owing to illness, or some other cause of absence on his part, the school was kept for a short time by Daniel Webster, then a student of law in Mr. Gore's office; and on this occasion, forty-seven or eight years ago, and I a child of ten, our acquaintance, since then never interrupted, began.

When I entered public life, it was with his encouragement. In 1838 I acted, fellow-citizens, as your organ in the great ovation which you gave him in this hall. When he came to the Department of State, in 1841, it was on his recommendation that I, living in the utmost privacy beyond the Alps, was appointed to a very high office abroad; and, in the course of the last year, he gave me the highest proof of his confidence, in intrusting to me the care of conducting his works through the press. May I venture, Sir, to add, that in the last letter but one which I had the happiness to receive from him, alluding, with a kind of sad presentiment, which I could not then fully appreciate, but which now unmans me, to these kindly relations of half a century, he adds, — "We now and then see stretching across the heavens a clear, blue, cerulean sky, without cloud, or mist, or haze. And such appears to me our acquaintance, from the time when I heard you for a week recite your lessons in the little school-house in Short Street to the date hereof," 21st July, 1852.

Mr. Chairman, I do not dwell upon the traits of

Mr. Webster's public character, however tempting the theme. Its bright developments, in a long life of service, are before the world; they are wrought into the annals of the country. Whoever, in after times, shall write the history of the United States for the last forty years, will write the life of Daniel Webster; and whoever writes the life of Daniel Webster as it ought to be written, will write the history of the Union from the time he took a leading part in its concerns. I prefer to allude to those private traits which show the MAN, the kindness of his heart, the generosity of his spirit, his freedom from all the bitterness of party, the unaffected gentleness of his nature. In preparing the new edition of his works, he thought proper to leave almost every thing to my discretion, as far as matters of taste are concerned. One thing only he enjoined upon me, with an earnestness approaching to a command. "My friend," said he, "I wish to perpetuate no feuds. I have lived a life of strenuous political warfare. I have sometimes, though rarely, and that in self-defence, been led to speak of others with severity; I beg you, where you can do it without wholly changing the character of the speech, and thus doing essential injustice to me, to obliterate every trace of personality of this kind. I should prefer not to leave a word that would give unnecessary pain to any honest man, however opposed to me."

But I need not tell you, fellow-citizens, that there is no one of our distinguished public men whose speeches contain less occasion for such an injunction. Mr. Webster habitually rejected the use of the poisoned weapons of personal invective or party odium. No one could more studiously abstain from all attempts to make a political opponent personally hateful. If the character of our Congressional discussions has of late years somewhat declined in dignity, no portion of the blame lies at his door. With Mr. Calhoun, who for a considerable portion of the time was his chief antagonist, and with whom he was brought into most direct collision, he maintained friendly personal relations. He did full justice to his talents and character. You remember the feeling with which he spoke of him at the time of his decease. Mr. Calhoun, in his turn, entertained a just estimate of his great opponent's worth. He said, toward the close of his life, that of all the leading men of the day, "there was not one whose political course had been more strongly marked by a strict regard to truth and honor than Mr. Webster's."

One of the resolutions speaks of a permanent memorial to Mr. Webster. I do not know what is contemplated, but I trust that such a memorial there will be. I trust that marble and brass, in the hands of the most skilful artists our country has produced, will be put in requisition to reproduce to us, — and nowhere so appropriately as in this hall, — the lineaments of that noble form and beaming countenance, on which we have so often gazed with delight. But, after all, fellow-citizens, the noblest monument must be found in his works. There he will live and speak to us and our children, when brass and marble have crumbled into dust. As a repository of political truth and practical wisdom, applied to the affairs of government, I know not where we shall find their equal. The works of Burke naturally suggest themselves to the mind, as the only writings in our language that can sustain the comparison. Certainly no compositions in the English tongue can take precedence of those of Burke, in depth of thought, reach of forecast, or magnificence of style. I think, however, it may be said without partiality, either national or personal, that while the reader is cloyed, at last, with the gorgeous finish of Burke's diction, there is a severe simplicity and a significant plainness in Webster's writing, that never tires. It is precisely this which characterizes the statesman, in distinction from the political philosopher. In political disquisition, elaborated in the closet, the palm must, perhaps, be awarded to Burke over all others, ancient or modern. But in the actual conflicts of the Senate, man against man, and opinion against opinion; in the noble war of debate, where measures are to be sustained and opposed, on which the welfare of the country and the peace of the world depend, where often the line of intellectual battle is changed in a moment; no time to reflect, no leisure to cull words, or gather up illustrations, but all to be decided by a vote, although the reputation of a life may be at stake, — all this is a very different matter, and here Mr. Webster was immeasurably the superior. Accordingly, we find, historically, (incredible as it sounds, and what I am ready to say I will not believe, though it is unquestionably true,) that these inimitable orations of Burke, which one cannot read without a thrill of admiration to his fingers' ends, actually emptied the benches of parliament.

Ah, gentlemen, it was very different with our great parliamentary orator. He not only chained to their seats willing, or, if there were such a thing, unwilling Senators, but the largest hall was too small for his audience. On the memorable 7th of March, 1850, when he was expected to speak upon the great questions then pending before the country, not only was the Senate Chamber thronged to its utmost capacity at an early hour, but all the passages to it, the Rotundo of the Capitol, and even the avenues of the city, were alive with the crowds who were desirous of gaining admittance. Another Senator, not a political friend, was entitled to the floor. With equal good taste and good feeling, he stated that "he was aware that the great multitude had not come together to hear him; and he was pleased to yield the floor to the only man, as he believed, who could draw together such an assembly." This sentiment, — the effusion of parliamentary courtesy, — will, perhaps, be found no inadequate expression of what will finally be the judgment of posterity.

Among the many memorable words which fell from the lips of our friend just before they were closed forever, the most remarkable are those which my friend Hillard has just quoted, "I STILL LIVE." They attest the serene composure of his mind, the Christian heroism, with which he was able to turn his consciousness in upon itself, and explore, step by step, the dark passage, (dark to us, but to him we trust already lighted from above,) which connects this world with the world to come. But I know not, Mr. Chairman, what words could have been better chosen to express his relation to the world he was leaving: "I still live. This poor dust is just returning to the dust from which it was taken; but I feel that I live in the affections of the people to whose service I have consecrated my days. I still live. The icy hand of death is already laid on my heart, but I shall still live in those words of faithful counsel which I have uttered to my fellow-citizens, and which I now leave them as the last bequest of a dying friend."

Mr. Chairman, in the long and honored career of our lamented friend there are efforts and triumphs which will hereafter fill one of the brightest pages in our history. But I greatly err if the closing scene — the height of the religious sublime — does not, in the judgment of other days, far transcend in interest the brightest exploits of public life. Within that darkened chamber at Marshfield, was witnessed a scene of which we shall not readily find the parallel. The serenity with which he stood in the presence of the King of Terrors, without trepidation or flutter, for hours and days of expectation; the thoughtfulness for the public business, when the sands were so nearly run out; the hospitable care for the reception of the friends who came to Marshfield; that affectionate and solemn leave separately taken, name by name, of wife, and children, and kindred, and friends, and family, down to the humblest members of the household; the designation of the coming day, then near at hand, when "all that was mortal of Daniel Webster would cease to exist;" the dimly-recollected strains of the funereal poetry of Gray, the last faint flash of the soaring intellect; the feebly murmured words of Holy Writ repeated from the lips of the good physician, who, when all the resources of human art had been exhausted, had a drop of spiritual balm for the parting soul; the clasped hands; the dying prayer. Oh! my fellow-citizens, that is a consummation over which tears of pious sympathy will be shed, ages after the glories of the Forum and the Senate are forgotten.

His sufferings ended with the day,
Yet lived he at its close;
And breathed the long, long night away,
In statue-like repose.

But ere the sun, in all his state,
Illumed the eastern skies,
He passed through glory's morning gate,
And walked in Paradise.

The resolutions were then adopted.

The Hon. WILLIAM APPLETON submitted the following resolve, which was likewise adopted:

Resolved, That as a token of respect for the memory of Mr. Webster, this meeting recommend that the banks, insurance offices, and other places of business be closed on Friday next.

The MAYOR announced the Committee of one hundred, as follows:

Thos. H. Perkins	John H. Pearson	Benjamin Loring
Geo. Ticknor	Samuel Hooper	Nathan Hale
Edward Everett	John P. Ober	Saml. A. Eliot
Nathan Appleton	Vernon Brown	William Appleton
Abbott Lawrence	J. Thos. Stevenson	William Amory
Benjamin Seaver	C. P. Curtis	Chas. H. Mills
Amos Lawrence	Chas. J. Hendee	A. Hemmenway
Francis C. Gray	James K. Mills	Francis Skinner
Samuel Lawrence	Francis C. Lowell	Chas. L. Woodbury

Robert G. Shaw	E. F. Raymond	Samuel Henshaw
John T. Heard	W. H. Larned	Benjamin F. Hallett
Franklin Haven	M. C. Barstow	Samuel Kettell
Chas. G. Greene	S. C. Allen	C. R. Ransom
Jno. C. Warren	Julius A. Palmer	Geo. Peabody
Jno. E. Thayer	Jno. C. Tucker	Thomas B. Wales
Thos. W. Ward	James Cheever	Samuel Whitwell
Jno. A. Lowell	Geo. B. Upton	P. W. Chandler
Saml. D. Bradford	Geo. R. Sampson	John W. Trull
Robert B. Storer	William Sturgis	James Whiting
Peter Harvey	Ozias Goodwin	Eliphalet Jones
Enoch Train	Paran Stevens	Silas Pearce
John M. Forbes	H. J. Gardner	Geo. W. Crockett
Levi A. Dowley	C. C. Felton	Andrew Carney
Moses Williams	Geo. T. Lyman	H. H. Hunnewell
Albert Fearing	H. M. Holbrook	James Lawrence
L. W. Tappan	Wm. T. Eustis.	J. W. James
Henry K. Horton	Thos. T. Whittemore	Jonas Chickering
Samuel T. Dana	William Almy	Peter Dunbar
W. W. Greenough	Joseph Packard	Arthur Pickering
Daniel Safford	N. A. Thompson	Henry Crocker
Jno. P. Thorndike	Chas. Larkin	Benjamin Smith
Wm. Hayden	Wm. Thomas	Ezra Forristall
Geo. T. Curtis	John Jeffries	Thomas B. Curtis
Jacob Sleeper	Amos A. Lawrence	

The meeting, after approving of this list of names, adjourned.

PROCEEDINGS

OF THE

CIRCUIT COURT OF THE UNITED STATES

FOR THE

DISTRICT OF MASSACHUSETTS.

PROCEEDINGS OF THE CIRCUIT COURT FOR THE DISTRICT OF MASSACHUSETTS.

THE members of the Bar met in the Law Library, Monday morning, October 25. They were called to order by the Hon. George Lunt, District Attorney of the United States, and Hon. Charles G. Loring was appointed Chairman, and Francis O. Watts, Esq., Secretary. Hon. Rufus Choate, Sydney Bartlett, Esq., Hon. George S. Hillard, Richard H. Dana, Jr., and George T. Curtis, Esquires, were appointed to report resolutions at a future meeting. Tuesday morning, at the adjourned meeting, Hon. Simon Greenleaf, John P. Putnam, and Tolman Willey, Esquires, were added to the committee. Thursday, October 28th, the Bar again met in the Supreme Court Room, and the resolutions given below were reported and adopted, when the meeting adjourned to the Circuit Court — then in session — CURTIS and SPRAGUE, Justices, on the bench. The room was crowded to overflowing. The Hon. GEORGE LUNT announced to the Court the death of Mr. Webster, as follows:

May it please your Honors — I have the sad duty to announce, as Attorney of the United States for this district, the removal of Daniel Webster, the great leader and exemplar of this Bar, by death. The performance of the mournful duty thus devolved upon me, results from my official position, and is in accordance with the usages of the Bar. But I should do dishonor to my own feelings, did I not at the same time signify that my heart beats in unison with all other hearts, under the pressure of so great a calamity. And, while I discharge this office, I only feel how inadequate must be every tribute of respect to the memory of that illustrious citizen, whose public life for so long a period has constituted one of the chief elements of the pride and glory of his country. But, feeling only too sensibly, that what belongs to me in this public expression of sorrow arises only from the accident of my position, I am equally sensible that it does not become me to assume the place of his eulogist, whose fame is indeed beyond all eulogy.

It is impossible not to be conscious that a glory has departed which blazes rarely in the successive centuries of time. And as in the disruption of private ties, we turn in vain to those who remain for relief, so in the departure of this great personage, singularly unequalled and unapproached by all others of his time, we feel that a vast and "aching void" will long be left unsatisfied in the beating heart of a nation.

But it is a source of satisfaction to me that there are present those members of this Bar who for many years have enjoyed the more intimate communion of this majestic spirit. They have been animated and elevated, and inspired by the sublime intellect of him whose record has long been written amongst

> The few, the immortal names,
> Which were not born to die.

To them I would respectfully leave what better becomes those who have nearer rights and higher capacities for so great a theme.

With the permission of your Honors, I will ask that, at the close of these proceedings, this Circuit Court of the United States do adjourn, and that the ceremonial of this day be entered upon its records.

The Hon. CHARLES G. LORING then addressed the court.

May it please the Court — I stand before you as the humble organ of this Bar, instructed to present for entry on your records resolutions passed at a recent meeting, expressive of our emotions upon the death of our illustrious leader, whose departure fills not only our, but a nation's heart with grief.

The subject, while of profoundest interest, is too grand for oratory. The announcement that Daniel Webster is dead fills the souls of all here with recollections, thoughts, and emotions, which no other words could excite. The simple statement of the event is the most appropriate eloquence. It is in justice only to ourselves, not to him, that our feelings seek utterance and relief in words.

His name and character, indeed, belong to the whole people of the United States of America, whom he has so long, so faithfully, and so gloriously served, and not to this, or any other Bar or State. There is not an intelligent citizen of this broad Republic, from the Canadas to the Rio Grande, or from the Atlantic to the Pacific, or who sails beneath its flag in the remotest sea, to whom knowledge of this event will not come as sad tidings of public calamity, — as of a tower of national strength laid low, as of a star stricken from the firmament of his country's glory.

The colossal grandeur of his intellect, the vast number and magnitude of his services as a patriotic statesman, and his rank as one of the most profound reasoners and sublime orators which have appeared in any age or nation; and the influences he has thus exercised, and for ages to come must continue to exert upon the mind, institutions, and destinies of the American people, are treasures of national wealth, and themes for other occasions.

But with these are inseparably connected his labors as a jurist, which it becomes us, more particularly, to commemorate on this occasion; and which, although less generally conspicuous, even to his contemporaries, and becoming less so as advancing time and experience consecrate into axioms the great principles which he was primarily and chiefly instrumental in establishing, are of no less magnitude and importance, as having led to those judicial constructions of the Constitution which have confirmed it in the confidence and affections of the people as a truly national institution. These services, we may, perhaps, be the more able to appreciate as presenting unequalled professional claims to the lasting gratitude of the country, and the admiration and reverence of every student of its judicial history.

To Mr. Webster are we chiefly indebted that the ægis of the National Constitution has been spread over the rights of property and franchises held under State charters, protecting them alike from oppressive, corrupt, or ill-considered local legislation; to him, for the first enunciation and maintenance of the great theory of the entire unity of the commercial relations of the several States, forbidding monopolies of any nature within the navigable waters of either; and to him, far beyond all others, in frequent political and forensic arguments, for those masterly expositions of the principles involved in the conflict of jurisdictions of the general government and of the individual States, which will henceforth compose, not so much weapons for conflict, as acknowledged truths upon which future questions shall be decided.

It is a common subject of thankfulness to the Divine Providence, which has hitherto so mercifully shaped our nation's destiny, that statesmen were originally vouchsafed capable of framing and administering our National Constitution; and it is no less a cause of reverential gratitude that, after they were gathered to their fathers, another was sent equally imbued with its spirit, and profound apprehension of its great principles, and their far-reaching influences, to apply them as a statesman and jurist in the great emergencies which were soon to arise, to test its adaptation to the vast ends for which it was designed.

And history, in completing the noblest column as yet raised in her temple, that of American constitutional liberty, while inscribing upon its tablet the names of Adams, Jefferson, Madison, Jay, and Hamilton, as founders of the glorious fabric, will instinctively add the name of Daniel Webster, as equally entitled to the eternal gratitude of his countrymen, as its expositor and defender. But to us, as members of this Bar, who have encountered or been associated with him in its arduous conflicts, have witnessed his forensic efforts, and enjoyed the privileges of social intercourse with him, and who have with such honest pride exulted in him as our head and leader, this event is of still closer interest. Who of us can ever forget his broad and comprehensive views, his clear and masterly statements of his cases, in themselves convincing arguments, the exquisite precision and no less wonderful language, his profound logic, his varied and extensive learning, his dignity of manner, and his matchless eloquence, his whole professional bearing? Who of us has failed to exult as we held our breath in his ascent as on eagles' wings to the highest heavens of eloquence, when conscious of the righteousness of his cause; or has not witnessed how heavy became his flight and drooping his pinions when conscious of a bad one? Mr. Webster could not, and all honor be to his name that he could not, argue a bad cause comparatively well. His mental vision was too penetrating and comprehensive, his logic too uncompromising, his perception of truth too clear, and his love of it too instinctive to fit him as the champion of error.

Well may we exclaim in retrospect of his intercourse and services at this Bar, —

Heu! quanto minus cum reliquis versari
Quam Tui meminisse.

But I forbear further allusion to our own bereavement. Standing, as we are, amid the ruins of a nation's fortress, the shock of whose fall is still vibrating throughout the land, the heart instinctively turns from the meditation of comparatively private sorrow to the nation's loss, and to gathering up the consolations of remembrance and hope. True, the mighty arm upon which we most confidently rested for defence against foreign political encroachment, and to maintain our dignity among the nations of the earth, is broken; the rock in the political wilderness which needed to be touched only by the wand of patriotism, to send forth gushing waters of wisdom and peace to allay the fever of the people, is removed out of its place; and the star that has so long guided in the night and tempest of national perplexity and agitation, is gone down forever; but the recorded treasures of his wisdom remain imperishable; the great principles he has established or vindicated for the nation's guidance, now become, and will forever stand as household gods in the hearts of the people. "I still live!" were the last words of the dying patriot, in prophetic vision of the immortality of his name and services; and he will "still live" in influence and grateful remembrance so long as the American Union shall endure, and its flag wave over an intelligent and loyal people.

Nor is the last and highest consolation wanting to us. Our friend died in the profession and peace of that faith which the greatest, equally with the humblest, needs in the scenes and labors of life, and in passing through the valley of the shadow of death, and yielded up his mighty spirit in filial trust to the God who gave it; who alone knoweth the heart and trieth the reins of man, and to whom alone, in faith and humility, must all judgment of our fellow-men, as well as of ourselves, be finally committed.

The Hon. George S. Hillard read the following resolutions of the Bar, and asked that they be entered upon the records of the Court.

Resolved, That as members of the Bar we look back with pride upon Mr. Webster's professional career, and acknowledge with gratitude the honor which such a life, and such powers, have shed upon the law. His mind was early imbued with the bracing learning of the common law, the principles of which he seized with a strong grasp, which neither time, nor subsequent devotion to pursuits of politics and government, ever relaxed. He was equally familiar with the technical refinements of special pleading, and the recondite learning of real law. Trained by long and constant conflict with some of the ablest lawyers and advocates whom this country has reared, his judgment in the conduct of causes, his familiarity with the rules of evidence, and his presence of mind in the meeting of legal emergencies, were not less conspicuous than the wisdom and eloquence which have made his public career so illustrious. His addresses to juries were marked by simplicity, clearness, dignity, and power. His legal arguments were learned, strong, luminous, and convincing. His profound and massive constitutional arguments embody the soundest principles of interpretation, and form unrivalled models of logical reasoning. His mind drew from the law no other elements than those of expansion and growth; and in the speeches and writings which have done so much honor to him, and so much honor to the country, we recognize the training and discipline derived from the studies and the contests of the Bar.

Resolved, That as citizens of our common country, we acknowledge, with profound sensibility, the great debt of gratitude and admiration due to him, as an enlightened and patriotic statesman. As a public man, he was just, brave, and wise; jealous of the honor of his own country, and mindful of the rights of others; far-seeing and sagacious — wise to discern the right, and firm in maintaining it. His political creed was the application of the rules of sound morals to government. He valued constitutional liberty because he understood it, and his powerful voice has penetrated wherever freedom was struggling and humanity oppressed. His views were broad, national, and comprehensive, limited to no party, and bounded by no section of the country. He detected with unrivalled sagacity the springs of national greatness, and expounded them with proportionate clearness and power. In counsels and principles like his, we see the elements of national power, of material prosperity, and of moral influence. Nor should we, in his more eminent and conspicuous merits, overlook the uniform dignity and decorum of his public career, the freedom from personality, and from appeals to low and unworthy motives, which characterize his speeches, and the high tone of thought and discussion which marks them.

Resolved, That we recognize in Mr. Webster's life and words, elements of greatness and power, independent of his career as a lawyer and a statesman. A writer, a thinker, and a speaker, his influence has been great while living, and will be not less great when dead. His vigorous and masculine style was no more than the adequate expression of weighty and striking thought. His eloquence was simple, severe, and grand, never stooping to exaggeration or extravagance, never lending itself to base or unworthy ends. His writings are treasures of thought, pure in their morality, of classical beauty, and ennobling in all their tendencies. His private life, not less than his public, illustrated the greatness of his character. In all his social and domestic relations, the varied and noble gifts of his intellect and of his heart shone conspicuously. The generous affections of friends, in which he was so rich, attest the integrity, uprightness, and beauty of his daily walk. And when Heaven decreed that he must close the majestic life which he had lived, he added to that life its crowning glory, by acknowledging his humble faith in the doctrines of Christianity, and by dying a Christian's death.

Resolved, That the Bar deeply mourn the loss of one so great as a statesman, so profound as a lawyer, and so noble as a man; that they tender their heartfelt sympathies to the family of the deceased, and request permission to join in the funeral ceremonies.

Resolved, That the President of this meeting be requested to communicate a copy of these Resolutions to the family of the deceased, and to present the same in the Circuit Court of the United States, now in session.

The Hon. RUFUS CHOATE then said:

May it please your Honors — I have been requested by the members of the Bar of this Court to add a few words to the resolutions just read, in which they have embodied, as they were able, their sorrow for the death of their beloved and illustrious member and countryman, Mr. Webster; their estimation of his character, life, and genius; their sense of the bereavement to the country, as to his friends, incapable of repair; the pride, the fondness, — the filial and the patriotic pride and fondness — with which they cherish, and would consign to history to cherish, the memory of a great and good man.

And yet, I could earnestly have desired to be excused from this duty. He must have known Mr. Webster less, and loved him less than your Honors, or than I have known and loved him, who can quite yet — quite yet — before we can comprehend that we have lost him forever — before the first paleness with which the news of his death overspread our cheeks has passed away; before we have been down to lay him in the Pilgrim soil he loved so well — till the heavens be no more — he must have known and loved him less than we have done — who can come here quite yet, to recount the series of his services — to display with psychological exactness the traits of his nature and mind; to ponder and speculate on the secrets, on the marvellous secrets and source of that vast power, which we shall see no more in action — nor aught in any degree resembling it — among men. These first moments should be given to grief. It may employ, it may promote, a calmer mood, to construct a more elaborate and less unworthy memorial.

For the purposes of this moment and place, indeed, no more is needed. What is there for this Court, or for this Bar, to learn from me, here and now of him? The year and the day of his birth — that birth-place on the frontier, yet bleak and waste; the well of which his childhood drank — dug by that father of whom he has said, "That through the fire and blood of seven years of revolutionary war, he shrank from no danger, no toil, no sacrifice, to serve his country, and to raise his children to a condition better than his own;" the elm tree that father planted, fallen now, as father and son have fallen; that training of the giant infancy, on Catechism and Bible, and Watts's version of the Psalms, and the traditions of Plymouth, and Fort William and Mary, and the Revolution, and the age of Washington and Franklin, on the banks of the Merrimack, flowing sometimes in flood and anger from his secret springs in the crystal hills; the two district schoolmasters, Chase and Tappan; the village library; the dawning of the love and ambition of letters; the few months at Exeter and Boscawen, the life of college, the probationary season of school-teaching, the clerkship in the Fryeburg Registry of Deeds; his admission to the Bar, presided over by judges like Smith, illustrated by practisers such as Mason, where, by the studies, in the contentions of nine years, he laid the foundation of the professional mind; his irresistible attraction to public life, the oration on Commerce, the Rockingham Resolutions, his first term of four years' service in Congress, when, by one bound, he sprang to his place by the side of the foremost of the rising American statesmen; his removal to this State, and then the double and parallel current in which his life, studies, thoughts, cares, have since flowed, bearing him to the leadership of the Bar by universal acclaim; bearing him to the leadership of public life; last of that surpassing triumvirate, shall we say the greatest, the most widely celebrated and admired; — all these things, to their minutest details, are known and rehearsed familiarly. Happier than the younger Pliny, happier than Cicero, he has found his historian, unsolicited, in his lifetime — and his countrymen have him all by heart!

There is, then, nothing to tell you; nothing to bring to mind. And then, if I may borrow the language of one of his historians and friends, one of those, through whose beautiful pathos the common sorrow uttered itself yesterday in Faneuil Hall — "I dare not come here, and dismiss, in a few summary paragraphs, the character of one who has filled such a space in the history, who holds such a place in the heart of his country. It would be a disrespectful familiarity, to a man of his lofty spirit, his great soul, his rich endowments, his long and honorable life, to endeavor thus to weigh and estimate them;" — a half-hour of words, a handful of earth, for fifty years of great deeds, on high places!

But although the time does not require any thing elaborated and adequate, — forbids it rather, — some broken sentences of veneration and love may be indulged to the sorrow which oppresses us.

There presents itself, on the first, and to any observation of Mr. Webster's life and character, a two-fold eminence; eminence of the very highest rank in a two-fold field of intellectual and public display, the profession of the law, and the profession of statesmanship, of which it would not be easy to recall any parallel in the biography of illustrious men.

Without seeking for parallels, and without asserting that they do not exist, consider that he was by universal designation the leader of the general American Bar; and that he was also by an equally universal designation foremost of her statesmen living at his death; inferior to not one who has lived and acted since the opening of his own public life. Look at these aspects of his greatness separately, — and from opposite sides of the surpassing elevation. Consider that his single career at the Bar may seem to have been enough to employ the largest faculties without repose, for a lifetime; and that if then and thus the "*infinitus forensium rerum labor*," should have conducted him to a mere professional reward — a Bench of Chancery or Law — the crown of the first of advocates — *jurisperitorum eloquentissimus* — to the pure and mere honors of a great magistrate; that that would be as much as is allotted to the ablest in the distribution of fame. Even that half — if I may say so — of his illustrious reputation — how long the labor to win it — how worthy of all that labor! He was bred first in the severest school of the common law, in which its doctrines were expounded by Smith, and its administration shaped and directed by Mason, — and its foundation principles, its historical sources and illustrations, its connection with the parallel series of statutory enactments, its modes of reasoning, and the evidence of its truths, he grasped easily and completely; and I have myself heard him say, that for many years while still at that Bar, he tried more causes and argued more questions of fact to the jury, than perhaps any other member of the profession anywhere. I have heard from others how even then he exemplified the same direct, clear, and forcible exhibition of proofs, and the reasonings appropriate to proofs — as well as the same marvellous power of discerning instantly what we call the decisive points of the cause in law and fact — by which he was later more widely celebrated. This was the first epoch in his professional training.

With the commencement of his public life, or with his later removal to this State, began the second epoch of his professional training — conducting him through the gradation of the national tribunals to the study and practice of the more flexible, elegant, and scientific jurisprudence of commerce and of chancery — and to the grander and less fettered investigations of international, prize, and constitutional law — and giving him to breathe the air of a more famous forum; in a more public presence; with more variety of competition, although he never met abler men, as I have many times heard him say, than some of those who initiated him in the rugged discipline of the

Courts of New Hampshire; and thus, at length, by these studies; these labors; this contention; continued without repose, he came, now many years ago, to stand *omnium assensu* at the summit of the American Bar.

It is common, and it is easy, in the case of all in such position, to point out other lawyers, here and there, as possessing some special qualification or attainment more remarkably, perhaps, because more exclusively;—to say of one that he has more cases in his recollection, at any given moment; or that he was earlier grounded in equity; or has gathered more black-letter or civil law; or knowledge of Spanish or Western titles; and these comparisons were sometimes made with him. But when you sought a counsel of the first-rate for the great cause, who would most surely discern and most powerfully expound the exact law, required by the controversy, in season for use—who could most skilfully encounter the opposing law, under whose power of analysis, persuasion, and display, the asserted right would assume the most probable aspect before the intelligence of the Judge; who, if the inquiry, became blended with, or resolved into facts, could most completely develop and most irresistibly expose them; one, "the law's whole thunder born to wield"—when you sought such a counsel, and could have the choice, I think the universal profession would have turned to him. And this would be so in nearly every description of cause, in any department. Some able men wield civil inquiries with a peculiar ability, some criminal. How lucidly and how deeply he unfolded a question of property you all know. But then, with what address, feeling, pathos, and prudence he defended; with what dignity and crushing power, *accusatorio spiritu*, he prosecuted the accused of crime, whom he believed to have been guilty, few have seen; but none who have seen can ever forget it.

Some scenes there are; some Alpine eminences rising above the high table-land of such a professional life, to which, in the briefest tribute, we should love to follow him. We recall that day, for an instance, when he first announced, with decisive display, what manner of man he was to the Supreme Court of the Nation. It was in 1818, and it was in the argument of the case of Dartmouth College. William Pinkney was recruiting his great faculties, and replenishing that reservoir of professional and elegant acquisition in Europe. Samuel Dexter, "the honorable man, and the counsellor, and the eloquent orator," was in his grave. The boundless old-school learning of Luther Martin; the silver voice and infinite analytical ingenuity and resource of Jones; the fervid genius of Emmett, pouring itself along *immenso ore;* the ripe and beautiful culture of Wirt and Hopkinson, the steel point unseen, not unfelt, beneath the foliage; Harper, himself, statesman as well as lawyer, these and such as these, were left of that noble Bar. That day Mr. Webster opened the cause of Dartmouth College to a tribunal unsurpassed on earth in all that gives illustration to a bench of law, not one of whom any longer survives.

One would love to linger on the scene—when, after a masterly argument of the law, carrying, as we may now know, conviction to the general mind of the court, and vindicating and settling for his lifetime his place in that forum, he paused to enter, with an altered feeling, tone, and manner, with these words on his peroration—"I have conducted my alma mater to this presence, that if she must fall, she may fall in her robes, and with dignity," and then broke forth in that strain of sublime and pathetic eloquence, of which we know not much more than that, in its progress, Marshall, the intellectual—the self-controlled—the unemotional, announced, visibly, the presence of the unaccustomed enchantment.

Other forensic triumphs crowd on us—in other competition—with other issues. But I must commit them to the historian of constitutional jurisprudence.

And now, if this transcendent professional reputation were all of Mr. Webster, it might be practicable, though not easy, to find its parallel elsewhere, in our own, or in European or classical biography.

But when you consider that side by side with this, there was growing up that other reputation—that of the first American statesman,—that for thirty-three years, and those embracing his most herculean works at the bar, he was engaged as a member of either House, or in the highest of the Executive departments, in the conduct of the largest national affairs—in the treatment of the largest national questions—in debate with the highest abilities of American public life—conducting diplomatic intercourse in delicate relations, with all manner of foreign powers—investigating whole classes of truths, totally unlike the truths of the law, and resting on principles totally distinct,—and that here, too, he was wise, safe, controlling, trusted, the foremost man; that Europe had come to see in his life a guaranty for justice, for peace, for the best hopes of civilization; and America to feel surer of her glory and her safety, as his great arm enfolded her—you see how rare, how solitary almost was the actual greatness! Who any where has won, as he had, the double fame, and worn the double wreath of Murray and Chatham, of Dunning and Fox, of Erskine and Pitt, of William Pinkney and Rufus King, in one blended and transcendent superiority?

I cannot attempt to grasp and sum up the aggregate of the service of his public life at such a moment as this—and it is needless. That life comprised a term of more than thirty-three years. It produced a body of performance, of which I may say generally, it was all which the first abilities of the country and time, employed with unexampled toil, stimulated by the noblest patriotism; in the highest places of the state—in the fear of God—in the presence of nations—could possibly compass.

He came into Congress after the war of 1812 had begun, and though probably deeming it unnecessary, according to the highest standards of public necessity, in his private character—and objecting, in his public character, to some of the details of the policy by which it was prosecuted, and standing by party ties in general opposition to the administration—he never breathed a sentiment calculated to depress the tone of the public mind; to aid or comfort the enemy; to check or chill the stirrings of that new, passionate, unquenchable spirit of nationality, which then was revealed, or kindled to burn till we go down to the tombs of States.

With the peace of 1815 his more cherished public labors began; and thenceforward has he devoted himself—the ardor of his civil youth—the energies of his maturest manhood—the autumnal wisdom of the ripened year—to the offices of legislation and diplomacy; of preserving the peace—keeping the honor—establishing the boundaries, and vindicating the neutral rights of his country—restoring a sound currency, and laying its foundations sure and deep—in upholding public credit—in promoting foreign commerce and domestic industry—in developing our uncounted material resources—giving the lake and the river to trade—and vindicating and interpreting the Constitution and the law. On all these subjects, on all measures practically in any degree affecting them, he has inscribed his opinions and left the traces of his hand. Everywhere the philosophical and patriot statesman and thinker will find that he has been before him,—lighting the way,—sounding the abyss. His weighty language, his sagacious warnings, his great maxims of empire, will be raised to view, and live to be deciphered when the final catastrophe shall lift the granite foundation in fragments from its bed.

In this connection I cannot but remark to how extraordinary an extent had Mr. Webster, by his acts, words, thoughts, or the events of his life, associated himself forever in the memory of all of us with every historical incident, or at least with every historical epoch; with every policy, with every glory, with every great name and fundamental institution, and grand or beautiful image, which are peculiarly and properly American. Look backwards to the planting of Plymouth and Jamestown, to the various scenes of colonial life in peace and war; to the opening, and march, and close of the revolutionary drama; to the age of the Constitution; to Washington, and Franklin, and Adams, and Jefferson; to the whole train of causes, from the Reformation downwards, which prepared us to be republicans,—to that other train of causes which led us to be unionists. Look round on field, workshop, and deck, and hear the music of labor rewarded, fed, and protected; look on the bright sisterhood of the States, each singing as a seraph in her motion, yet blending in a common harmony, and there is nothing which does not bring him, by some tie, to the memory of America. We seem to see his form and hear his deep, grave speech everywhere. By some felicity of his personal life; by some wise, deep, or beautiful word, spoken or written; by some service of his own, or some commemoration of the services of others, it has come to pass that "our granite hills, our inland seas, and prairies, and fresh, unbounded, magnificent wilderness;" our encircling ocean; the rock of the Pilgrims; our new-born sister of the Pacific; our popular assemblies; our free schools; all our cherished doctrines of education, and of the influence of religion, and material policy, and the law, and the Constitution, give us back his name. What American landscape will you look on; what subject of American interest will you study; what source of hope or of anxiety, as an American, will you acknowledge, that it does not recall him?

I shall not venture in this rapid and general recollection of Mr. Webster, to attempt to analyze that intellectual power which all admit to have been so extraordinary, or to compare or contrast it with the mental greatness of others—in variety or degree—of the living or the dead; or even to appreciate exactly, and in reference to canons of art, his single attribute of eloquence. Consider, however, the remarkable phenomenon of excellence in three unkindred, one might have thought, incompatible forms of public speech—that of the forum, with its double audience of bench and jury, of the halls of legislation, and of the most thronged and tumultuous assemblies of the people. Consider, further, that this multiform eloquence, exactly as his words fell, became at once so much accession to permanent literature, in the strictest sense—solid, attractive, and rich—and ask how often in the history of public life such a thing has been exemplified. Recall what pervaded all these forms of display, and every effort in every form, that union of naked intellect in its largest measure, which penetrates to the exact truth of the matter in hand by intuition or by inference, and discerns every thing which may make it intelligible, probable, or credible to another, with an emotional and moral nature profound, passionate, and ready to kindle, and with an imagination enough to supply a hundred-fold more of illustration and aggrandizement than his taste suffered him to accept; that union of greatness of soul with depth of heart, which made his speaking almost more an exhibition of character than of mere genius; the style not merely pure, clear Saxon, but so constructed, so numerous as far as becomes prose, so forcible, so abounding in unlabored felicities, the words so choice, the epithet so pictured, the matter absolute truth, or the most exact and specious resemblance the human wit can devise, the treatment of the subject, if you have regard to the kind of truth he had to handle, political, ethical, legal, as deep, as complete as Paley's, or Locke's, or Butler's, or Alexander Hamilton's, of their subjects; yet that depth and that completeness of sense, made transparent as through crystal waters, all embodied in harmonious or well-composed periods, raised on winged language, vivified, fused, and poured along in a tide of emotion, fervid and incapable to be withstood—recall the form, the eye, the brow, the tone of voice, the presence of the intellectual king of men—recall him thus, and in the language of Mr. Justice Story, commemorating Samuel Dexter, we may well "rejoice that we have lived in the same age, that we have listened to his eloquence, and been instructed by his wisdom."

I cannot leave the subject of his eloquence without returning to a thought I have advanced already. All that he has left—or the larger portion of all—is the record of spoken words. His works, as already collected, extend to many volumes—a library of reason and eloquence, as Gibbon has said of Cicero's—but they are volumes of speeches only, or mainly; and yet who does not rank him as a great American author—an author as truly expounding, and as characteristically exemplifying in a pure, genuine, and harmonious English style, the mind, thought, point of view of objects, and essential nationality of his country, as any other of our authors, professionally so denominated? Against the maxim of Mr. Fox, his speeches read well, and yet were good speeches—great speeches in the delivery. For so grave were they; so thoughtful and true; so much the eloquence of reason at last; so strikingly always they contrived to link the immediate topic with other and broader principles, ascending easily to widest generalizations; so happy was the reconciliation of the qualities which engage the attention of hearers, yet reward the perusal of students, so critically did they keep the right side of the line which parts eloquence from rhetoric, and so far do they rise above the penury of mere debate, that the general reason of the country has enshrined them at once, and forever, among our classics.

It is a common belief that Mr. Webster was a various reader; and I think it is true, even to a greater degree than has been believed. In his profession of politics, nothing I think, worthy of attention, had escaped him, nothing of the "ancient or modern prudence," nothing which Greek or Roman, or European speculation in that walk had explored, or Greek or Roman, or European or universal history, or public biography exemplified. I shall not soon forget with what admiration he spake, at an interview to which he admitted me while in the Law School at Cambridge, of the politics and ethics of Aristotle, and of the mighty mind which, as he said, seemed to have "thought through" so many of the great problems which form the discipline of social man. American history, and American political literature he had by heart,—the long series of influences which trained us for representative and free government; that other series of influences, which moulded us into a united government; the Colonial era; the age of controversy before the Revolution; every scene, and every person in that great tragic action; every question which has successively engaged our politics, and every name which has figured in them, — the whole stream of our time was open, clear, and present ever to his eye.

Beyond his profession of politics, so to call it, he had been a diligent and choice reader, as his extraordinary style in part reveals, and I think the love of reading would have gone with him to a later and riper age, if to such an age it had been the will of God to reserve him. This is no place or time to appreciate this branch of his acquisitions; but there is an interest inexpressible in knowing who were any of the chosen from among the great dead in the library of such a man. Others may correct me, but I should say of that interior and narrower circle, were Cicero, Virgil, Shakspeare — whom he knew familiarly as the Constitution — Bacon, Milton, Burke, Johnson — to whom, I hope it is not pedantic nor fanciful to say, I often thought his nature presented some resemblance; the same "abundance of the general propositions required for explaining a difficulty and refuting a sophism, copiously and promptly occurring to him;" the same kindness of heart, and wealth of sensibility; under a manner, of course, more courteous and gracious, yet more sovereign; the same sufficient, yet not predominant imagination, stooping ever to truth, and giving affluence, vivacity, and attraction, to a powerful, correct, and weighty style of prose.

I cannot leave this life and character, without selecting and dwelling a moment on one or two of his traits, or virtues, or felicities, a little longer. There is a collective impression made by the whole of an eminent person's life, beyond and other than, and apart from that which the mere general biographer would afford the means of explaining. There is an influence of a great man derived from things indescribable almost, or incapable of enumeration, or singly insufficient to account for it; but through which his spirit transpires, and his individuality goes forth on the contemporary generation. And thus, I should say, one grand tendency of his life and character was to elevate the whole tone of the public mind. He did this, indeed, not merely by example. He did it by dealing as he thought, truly, and in manly fashion, with that public mind. He evinced his love of the people, not so much by honeyed phrases, as by good counsels and useful service, *vera pro gratis*. He showed how he appreciated them, by submitting sound arguments to their understandings, and right motives to their free will. He came before them less with flattery than with instruction; less with a vocabulary larded with the words, humanity, and philanthrophy, and progress, and brotherhood, than with a scheme of politics, an educational, social, and governmental system, which would have made them prosperous, happy, and great.

What the greatest of the Greek historians said of Pericles, we all feel might be said of him, "He did not so much follow as lead the people, because he framed not his words to please them, like one who is gaining power by unworthy means, but was able and dared the on strength of his high character, even to brave their anger by contradicting their will."

I should indicate it as another influence of his life, acts, and opinions, that it was in an extraordinary degree uniformly and liberally conservative. He saw with vision as of a prophet, that if our system of united government can be maintained till a nationality shall be generated of due intensity and due comprehension, a glory indeed millennial, a progress without end, a triumph of humanity hitherto unseen, were ours; and therefore he addressed himself to maintain that united government.

Standing on the rock of Plymouth, he bade distant generations hail, and saw them rising, "demanding life, impatient for the skies," from what were "fresh, unbounded, magnificent wildernesses," — from the shore of the great tranquil sea, — not yet become ours. But observe to what he welcomes them, by what he would bless them. "It is to good government;" it is to "treasures of science, and delights of learning;" it is to the "sweets of domestic life, the immeasurable good of rational existence, the immortal hopes of Christianity, the light of everlasting truth."

It will be happy, if the wisdom and temper of his administration of our foreign affairs shall preside in the time which is at hand. Sobered, instructed by the examples and warnings of all the past, he yet gathered from the study and comparison of all the eras, that there is a silent progress of the race, without pause, without haste, without return, to which the counsellings of history are to be accommodated by a wise philosophy. More than, or as much as that of any of our public characters, his statesmanship was one which recognized a Europe, an old world, but yet grasped the capital idea of the American position, and deduced from it the whole fashion and color of its policy; which discerned that we are to play a high part in human affairs, but discerned also what part it is, peculiar, distant, distinct, and grand as our hemisphere; an influence, not a contact, — the stage, the drama, the catastrophe, all but the audience all our own; and if ever he felt himself at a loss, he consulted reverently the genius of Washington.

In bringing these memories to a conclusion, for I omit many things because I dare not trust myself to speak of them, I shall not be misunderstood, or give offence, if I hope that one other trait in his public character, one doctrine, rather, of his political creed, may be remembered and be appreciated. It is one of the two fundamental precepts in which Plato, as expounded by the great master of Latin eloquence and reason and morals, comprehends the duty of those who share in the conduct of the state, — "*Ut, quæcunque agunt, TOTUM corpus reipublicæ curent; nedum partem aliquam tuentur, reliquas deserant,*" that they comprise in their care the whole body of the republic, nor keep one part and desert another. He gives the reason, one reason, of the precept, — "*Qui autem parti civium consulunt, partem negligunt, rem perniciosissimam in civitatem inducunt, seditionem atque discordiam.*" The patriotism which embraces less than the whole, induces sedition and discord, the last evil of the state.

How profoundly he had comprehended this truth; with what persistency, with what passion, from the first hour he became a public man, to the last beat of the great heart, he cherished it; how little he accounted the good, the praise, the blame, of this locality or that, in comparison of the larger good, and the general and thoughtful approval of his own and our whole America, she this day feels and announces. Wheresoever a drop of her blood flows in the veins of man, this trait is felt and appreciated. The hunter beyond Superior, the fisherman on the deck of the nigh night-foundered skiff, the sailor on the uttermost sea, will feel, as he hears these tidings, that the protection of a sleepless, all-embracing parental care, is withdrawn from him for a space, and that his pathway henceforward is more solitary and less safe than before.

But I cannot pursue these thoughts. Among the eulogists who have just uttered the eloquent sorrow of England at the death of the great Duke, one has employed an image, and an idea, which I venture to modify and appropriate.

"The Northmen's image of death is finer than that of other climes; no skeleton, but a gigantic figure that envelops men within the massive folds of its dark garment. Webster seems so enshrouded from us, as the last of the mighty Three, themselves following a mighty series; the greatest closing the procession. The robe draws round him, and the era is past."

Yet how much there is which that all-ample fold shall not hide;—the recorded wisdom; the great example; the assured immortality.

They speak of monuments!

> Nothing can cover his high fame but heaven,
> No pyramids set-off his memories
> But the eternal substance of his greatness;
> To which I leave him.

George T. Curtis, Esq., followed Mr. Choate:

May it please your Honors—In the general sorrow which pervades all hearts, perhaps the consoling reflections which I am able to bring from the last earthly presence of the great departed will find appropriate expression here.

We have all witnessed his life. We have known him in the Senate, in the forum, in the popular assembly, in the social circle; in all the works and the duties of the manifold relations which he filled with his own peculiar greatness.

It was my privilege, also, to have witnessed his *death*, so *grand*, so *tranquil*, that we who stood and watched the moments that were slowly bearing away from us his great spirit, could scarcely feel the weight of the affliction which was descending upon our souls, and when in the silence of that chamber, which the breath of an infant would have broken, the dread announcement came at last, we seemed to have watched, and served, and prayed, not at a dissolution of this "mortal coil," but at a translation of some great servant of God into the realms of bliss.

It is known to all that the death of Mr. Webster was, in all respects, worthy of his life. It was more. It was the consummation of his character, the crowning glory of his whole mortal existence. It was his singular happiness to have been able to approach the dark portals of the tomb with a perfectly distinct and clear perception, that they had been opened to receive him; and yet with his mind under its own entire control, as completely as it had ever been, since it came from his Maker's hands.

The manner in which he kept himself in a perfectly elevated, noble, and religious state of mind, and yet never lost sight of the smallest duties, or failed in the expression of a kind thought to those about him, seemed to me to mark the greatness of his nature, more than all the other proofs of intellectual supremacy which his life has exhibited. His vast intellect never changed its relations to any subject, any thing, or any person; never lost the sense of what was due to his own character and his own position among men; never withdrew itself from a single occupation; never exchanged the activity of life for the imbecilities of disease; never yielded to complaint; never surrendered itself to aught but the final grasp of death, which shut it from earthly manifestation.

In all this extraördinary exhibition of the power and balance of his mind, there was nothing of Roman stoicism. A more than Roman dignity enveloped him to the end. His warm affections remained unchanged, overflowing to all around him; and he could not so have died if he had not been sustained by a religious faith, such a mind like his must possess if it lives at all. There was nothing in his faith of a technical character. No expression escaped him which would mark him as of this or that theology, or of any church, save the universal church of Christ. "What," said he, to those who gathered about him, "what would be the condition of any of us without the hope of immortality?"

What is there to rest that hope upon but the Gospel? And it was while resting his hope upon that foundation that he could look back over his long life and say,—"My general wish on earth has been to do my Maker's will. I thank him. I thank him for the means of doing some little good for these beloved objects, for the blessings that surround me, for my nature and associations. I thank him that I am to die under so many circumstances of love and affection." It was his good fortune, also,—in which, considering how far from that spot his public duties considerably drew him, we may see almost a special Providence,—that he died in the home of his affections, and away from all the scenes and exactions of political strife.

There his last days, and even hours, were given peacefully to the great concerns of his country, from which his attention was never withdrawn, until the messenger from another world was actually at the door. There he found solace to his declining strength, amid the scenes of nature which he so passionately loved, and in which he had been so long accustomed to renew his power.

There were the graves of the loved and lost who had gone before him; there was the beautiful home, which his fame has made historical, and which he fondly trusted would remain to his blood and name through the generations that still gather around its hearth. There his great heart could expand itself to the love of those nearest and dearest to him on earth, and there he could receive as he did receive from those not present as well as from those who were about him, a ministry of veneration and love which will be to them a precious recollection forever.

Mr. Justice Sprague replied:

The event we deplore is solemn, is appalling, not only as a calamity and for the void which it creates, but still more as bringing with it an overwhelming sense of the nothingness of human power. Others may have excelled Mr. Webster in some intellectual endowment, but in the combination of the statesman, the orator, the diplomatist, the jurist, and the advocate, the present age has produced no equal, and no age a superior.

It was my lot to be associated with him in both branches of the National Legislature, and as a member of the same political party, of the same profession, and from the same section of the country. It is now nearly twenty-seven years since I entered the House of Representatives, of which he was then a member. The preëminence asserted for him by his friends, was not then conceded by his opponents. But it was soon observable that whenever a debate arose in which Mr. Webster took an earnest part, even those who were most strenuous in denying his general superiority, were constrained to admit that upon that occasion he had excelled all others. These occasions at length became so multiplied, with so many opponents, and upon such a variety of topics, that in spite of sectional jealousy, of party prejudice and intolerance, and of personal partialities and local pride, the admission of his superiority was forced upon unwilling minds, and from reluctant lips, and he stood confessed by all unequalled in intellectual power. In the most violent times, under the most exasperating attacks, personal and political, he never transcended the limits of good taste or parliamentary decorum—never violated the courtesy and dignity of senatorial debate.

Should any be disposed to say of him as was said of Burke—

> Born for the universe, he narrowed his mind,
> And to party gave up what was meant for mankind,

it should be answered also, that what he gave to party he gave to mankind; for he established principles and elucidated truths of universal application and eternal duration.

No man can read his speeches without clearer views upon great political problems, without a more profound comprehension of the true foundation upon which civil society should be erected, and the just rules by which its affairs should be conducted.

No candid mind can rise from the perusal of his works without a more just and elevated appreciation of our own Constitution and Government, a warmer and more exalted patriotism, without being a truer and firmer friend of real republicanism, of justice, of law, of order, of universal regulated liberty.

The present occasion does not permit me to verify these general remarks by specific and detailed references, nor has the time arrived when his later efforts can be dispassionately considered.

But there is one speech made, so long since as to be now matter of history, and involving no topic of personal excitement, of which I have been especially requested to speak, because it is the most celebrated, and of the then Senators from New England, I am, with one exception, the only survivor; and it is proper to speak of it here and now, because a great vital question of constitutional law was by that speech settled as completely and irrevocably as it could have been by the greatest minds in the highest judicial tribunals.

Mr. Foot's resolutions involved merely the question of limiting or extending the survey of the public lands. Upon this, Mr. Benton and Mr. Hayne addressed the Senate, condemning the policy of the Eastern States, as illiberal towards the West. Mr. Webster replied, in vindication of New England and the policy of the Government. It was then that General Hayne made the assault which that speech repelled.

It has been asked if it be possible that that reply was made without previous preparation. There could have been no special preparation before the speech began to which it was an answer. When General Hayne closed, Mr. Webster followed, with the interval only of the usual adjournment of one night.

His reply was made to repel an attack, sudden, unexpected, and almost unexampled, an attack upon Mr. Webster personally, upon Massachusetts and New England, and upon the Constitution.

There can be little doubt that this attack was the result of premeditation, concert, and arrangement. His assailant selected his own time, and that too, peculiarly inconvenient to Mr. Webster, for at that moment the Supreme Court were proceeding in the hearing of a cause of great importance, in which he was leading counsel. For this reason, he requested, through a friend, a postponement of the debate. General Hayne objected, and the request was refused. The assailant, too, selected his own ground, and made his choice of topics, without reference to the resolution before the Senate, or the legitimate subject of debate. The time, the matter, and the manner, indicate that the attack was made with a design to crush a formidable political opponent. To this end, personal history, the annals of New England and of the federal party were ransacked for materials. It was attempted to make him responsible, not only for what was his own, but for the opinions and conduct of others. All the errors and delinquencies, real or supposed, of Massachusetts and the Eastern States, and of the federal party, during the war of 1812, and throughout their history, were to be accumulated on him. It was supposed, that, as a representative, he would be driven to attempt to defend what was indefensible, and to uphold what could not be sustained, and as a federalist, to oppose the popular resolutions of '98.

Gen. Hayne heralded his speech with a declaration of war, with taunts and threats, vaunting anticipated triumph, as if to paralyze by intimidation ; saying that he had something rankling in his breast, and that he would carry the war into Africa, until he had obtained indemnity for the past, and security for the future.

Mr. Webster evidently felt the magnitude of the occasion, and a consciousness that he was more than equal to it. On no other occasion, although I have heard him hundreds of times, have I seen him so thoroughly aroused. Yet when he commenced, and throughout the whole, he was perfectly self-possessed and self-controlled. Never was his bearing more lofty, his person more majestic, his manner more appropriate and impressive.

At first a few of his opponents made some show of indifference. But the power of the orator soon swept away all affectation, and a solemn, deep, absorbing interest was manifested by all, and continued even through his profound discussion of Constitutional law.

When he closed, the impression upon all was too deep for utterance, and, to this day, no one who was present has spoken of that speech but as a matchless achievement and a complete triumph. When he sat down, General Hayne arose, and endeavored to restate and reënforce his argument. This instantly called forth from Mr. Webster that final, condensed reply which has the force of a moral demonstration.

The value of that speech cannot be measured, without a just appreciation of our Constitution, and of republican government. Nullification had become formidable. It had been practically adopted in high places, and was sustained by several States, and some of the ablest minds of the South, and was daily gaining strength, as the offspring of the resolutions of '98. By this single effort that deadly heresy was prostrated and crushed forever.

No speech, ancient or modern, has within the same time convinced so many minds, and produced so great and salutary results. It was not addressed merely to the enlightened and reflecting audience around him, but to this great reading nation, and to the civilized world. If the doctrines of General Hayne had prevailed, this Union would have been shattered into fragments; but Mr. Webster and his doctrines have triumphed, and our Union remains, in all its magnificence and beneficence.

When Mr. Webster first entered the State Department, our foreign affairs, particularly with Great Britain, were complicated and critical in the extreme. Adverse military forces had been gathered upon our north-eastern boundary. In relation to the affair of the Caroline, an unsound doctrine of international law had been put forth on our part, which, if it had been carried out by the threatened punishment of the soldier McLeod, would immediately have brought a hostile fleet upon our coast. The matter of the Creole, too, was a further disturbing cause. Mr. Webster extricated the Government from the false position in which it had been placed by his predecessor, by frankly conceding what we could not justly maintain, and planting himself only upon the right.

His state papers, during the administration of Harrison and Tyler, are unsurpassed in power, truth, and propriety. His diplomacy was consummate. It attained complete success, and entitled him to the gratitude of his country and the world. If his principles and practice should be followed by all nations, war would cease, and the reign of peace be universal.

Men distinguished in political life have often attempted in vain to command success at the bar, while great lawyers have signally failed in a parliamentary career. Distinct powers are required for each. For the one, the power of resolving a question into its elements; and for the other, the power of combination, of dealing with masses, and of holding great subjects in a comprehensive grasp. Mr. Webster possessed both, preëminently.

As a lawyer, he for nearly thirty years stood at the head of the Bar of the United States, without a rival; while, at the same time, he maintained his pre-eminence as a statesman and an orator, in the halls of Congress, or at the head of a Cabinet. In consultation, no man was more weighty; in trials at the bar, no man was his equal. He possessed every requisite for success in the highest degree. Eloquent, sagacious, fearless, circumspect, ready, learned, and profound. No other lawyer has so ably expounded the Constitution, and no one has done so much to maintain it upon its true foundation, and in its just proportions. Superior as he must have felt himself to be, to those whom he generally addressed, that superiority was never asserted in his manner towards the bench, which was uniformly respectful and deferential. He wished the law to be revered, and he knew that reverence for it could not be maintained without respect for the tribunals by which it is administered. Faithful to his clients, he was also true to the court, and never, for temporary success, exerted his great powers to subvert fundamental principles, or confound the rules of right. He never used his gigantic strength to remove the landmarks of the law. He dealt with facts as an advocate, but with the law as a jurist. It was with him a science, upon which depended public and private right, social order, the peace, the existence of civilized society. I leave to the learned Justice of the Supreme Court, who has been so recently and intimately associated with him at the bar, to present a more complete delineation of his forensic character.

Extraordinary as were the natural gifts of the great departed, he did not trust to them alone. He was laborious, but not with incessant toil. He gave himself frequent intervals of relaxation and repose; but when his mind was brought into earnest exercise, it worked with an intensity and effect that could not be exceeded. One part of his intellectual training particularly recommends itself to the young men of his own profession. When any question was presented to his mind, he was not content to examine it only to see what could be said on his own side, or to maintain a thesis, but he investigated the subject on all sides, sounded its depths, explored its foundations, and having found the truth, laid it up as a treasure to be kept forever. It was thus that he amassed amazing intellectual wealth, upon which he could draw at any time as an exhaustless mine. He had a profound respect and reverence for the Christian religion and its ordinances. Whenever he spoke of them it was in deep tones of solemnity and awe. No one who knew him would presume to speak of them lightly or thoughtlessly in his presence.

I had hoped that when the time should have arrived for his withdrawal from the active scenes of political life, he would, in his rural retreat, have devoted his last years to the investigation and contemplation of the momentous subject of revelation and a future life, and that he would have given to the world the fruits of the inquiries and reflections of his great mind. Such a work would have been of transcendent value, and a graceful close, and the crowning glory of the labors of his life. But Infinite Wisdom and

Infinite Goodness have ordered it otherwise, and we have only to bow in humble submission to the dispensation.

Mr. Justice CURTIS said:

I receive with deep sensibility the resolutions of the Bar, and the remarks of yourself, Mr. Attorney, and of the other gentlemen who have addressed us. The death of this illustrious statesman and jurist has produced a profound impression everywhere in the country to whose service he devoted his life, and will be felt as an event not unimportant in the civilized world.

Among the gentlemen of this Bar, of which he was a member, with very many of whom he held relations of private friendship, and for whom, as a body, he was ever ready to manifest a fraternal regard, and in this Court, which, for more than thirty years, he has enlightened and assisted by his labors, a deep feeling of private grief mingles itself with our sense of the public loss. How great this loss is cannot be described, for it cannot now be even known. The darkness of the future covers the dangers which the Providence of God may permit our country to encounter, and hides from view our needs for the patriotism and surpassing mental power of Mr. Webster. In a government depending for its existence on opinion, the withdrawal of a mind which exercised so great an influence for the preservation and stability of our country, not only in the public councils, but among the people themselves, is a loss indeed.

We submit ourselves to it as inevitable, as having

come at the time appointed by the will of Him in whose hand is the destiny of nations, and of men, and with gratitude that so much has been accomplished by him, and so much left for the instruction of this and future times. Of his services and works as a statesman, I can say nothing after what others have said.

But receiving these communications from his brethren of the Bar, I am strongly reminded of the importance to them of the memory and fame of this great lawyer. The illustrious names and great deeds which centuries have gathered are the richest treasures of a nation. The master-pieces of literature and art dignify the pursuits in which they were produced.

We may claim Daniel Webster as an American lawyer. Born during the War of the Revolution, in a family which took an honorable part in that great struggle, he was imbued from his infancy with American ideas and principles. He was reared in the simple habits of a New England home. He was forced early into the rough and invigorating contact with nature among the mountains where he had his birthplace. He was trained in the college of his native State. He studied our common law; for although it was painfully wrought out from age to age in another land, yet it was by our ancestors, and I thank God that by as good a title as can be shown under its rules, it is our healthy and manly intellectual, as well as political, inheritance. He knew it as it is in Littleton, this his great commentator, and in Plowden and Saunders, as well as in its more modern sources. His mind was imbued with its logic, and its peculiar style was as familiar to him as that of Taylor or Milton. Its fundamental principles had become a part of the structure of his mind, and under these new skies he maintained and advanced those great principles of personal liberty under the law and by the law, and the absolute security of private property, which constitute the vital power of the common law. But it must not be forgotten, for the honor of American jurisprudence, and for his honor, that he entered a field such as has existed nowhere else in any age.

It was and is one of the excellencies of the Constitution of the United States that it did not attempt too much, that it is neither a treatise nor a code, but a simple enumeration of the great powers and principles necessary to constitute the government of our country. When this government was put into operation in the same territory and over the same people, having distinct State governments of their own, questions of the last importance to the tranquillity and peace of the country, and to the efficiency and success of the new government, necessarily arose. Few men, whose attention has not been particularly directed to this subject, are aware of the number, the importance, or the difficulty of these questions. A country, already vast in extent, and whose resources, in a rapid course of development, were incalculable; whose people, after great suffering, had, by their own acts, become a nation, had created a court of justice, and delegated to it the power, and imposed upon it, under the most solemn sanctions, the duty of declaring void all legislative acts not in conformity with the Constitution, and of restraining within their appropriate limits of power the State sovereignties under which the people lived.

Questions which elsewhere could have been settled only by mere force, or by diplomatic negotiations, which force influences, were here to be brought to an arbitrament, according to the staid, settled, and regular course of judicial procedure.

Into these contests Mr. Webster entered, and for them he was fitted, I think, as no other man has been. He brought to these great debates extensive and accurate historical learning, especially concerning the Constitution itself; a clearness of conception, comprehensiveness of grasp, and logical power never surpassed; and to all these was added a command of the English tongue, which, for demonstrative oratory, has, I think, not been equalled.

We may all conceive, what many yet know, that he was able to render, and did render to his country, and to the cause of justice and peace, the most eminent service, in this unobtrusive but important scene of action. And we shall make but poor use of his great example if we do not borrow from it higher conceptions and broader views of the capacities and duties of his and our profession. Of even the most prominent causes of great and permanent public importance in which Mr. Webster was engaged, there is not time here to speak, but it may be said generally, without doing any injustice to the great magistrates by whom they were determined, what indeed they were ever ready to acknowledge, that they derived most important assistance from the labors of Mr. Webster.

It is the general destiny of lawyers to leave behind them but few traces, and no monuments, of their intellectual labor. Eloquence and learning, and devotion to duty, and strenuous effort, and high courage, serve their uses of the day, and doubtless find their regard in the breast of their possessor, but with him often dies even their memory. How little do we know of the forensic arguments of Ames, or Dexter, or Otis. Vague impressions of their power still linger on the fleeting recollections of a few living men, to depart, when they go home, and leave no trace behind.

To a very considerable extent Mr. Webster will probably not partake of this ordinary lot of his brethren. Many of his forensic arguments have been made in causes of such great and permanent importance, they are so admirable in themselves, and in general have been so well preserved, that they may be expected to be recurred to and studied while the Constitution shall endure.

What estimate posterity may form of the importance to them of this part of his labors, it would be presumptuous in us to attempt to decide. But for ourselves we can declare, that he who has strengthened the foundations of the Constitution, and shielded it from hostile attack, and made apparent to the affections of the people, the strength and beauty of its proportions and the peace and safety which are to be found only within its walls, has rendered to us a service not lightly to be esteemed or soon forgotten.

That in this I do but feebly express what this nation now feels, no man can doubt. To what has been so eloquently said at the Bar concerning his life and his death, it cannot be necessary that I should express my assent. But I desire to say, what I strongly feel and what it must gratify every man who loves his country to feel, that the death of Mr. Webster has given us a new and affecting proof that we are indeed one people, united by a common attachment to our country and to its great institutions and principles, and to the men who represent and uphold them; that underneath the strife of parties and the more miserable contests of sections and factions, deep in the American heart is a love of the whole country, and therefore it is that from that heart has come the utterances of grief, which arise everywhere over this broad land; grief for the loss of the man whose heart was large enough, and whose mind was comprehensive enough to include this Union, with all its interests and dependencies, and opinions, and obligations, and rights. And the great principles which he had so powerfully taught in his life, receive from his death a new sanction by his countrymen.

PROCEEDINGS

IN THE

SUPREME JUDICIAL COURT

OF

MASSACHUSETTS.

PROCEEDINGS IN THE SUPREME JUDICIAL COURT OF MASSACHUSETTS.

THIS Court was holding the Law Term at Taunton, in Bristol county. There were present Chief Justice SHAW, and Justices DEWEY, METCALF, BIGELOW, and CUSHING.

A meeting of the Bar was held October 26; Hon. Charles J. Holmes, of Fall River, was chosen Chairman, and Jacob H. Loud, of Plymouth, was appointed Secretary. A Committee of seven was appointed by the Chair, to take such order, and report such resolutions, as would express the sentiments of the Bar on occasion of the demise of the late Honorable Daniel Webster; and Messrs. Coffin of New Bedford, Whitman of Abington, G. Marston of Barnstable, Colby of New Bedford, Farnsworth of Pawtucket, Eliot of New Bedford, and Miller of Wareham, were appointed said Committee.

The Committee presented the following Resolutions, which were unanimously adopted.

The members of the Bar of the Old Colony, composed of the counties of Bristol, Plymouth, Barnstable, and Dukes County, having learned with the most profound sorrow the decease of the

Honorable Daniel Webster, avail themselves of this earliest opportunity, at their Annual Meeting at the Law Term of the Supreme Judicial Court, now held at Taunton, to express the sentiments which they entertain, in common with the whole country, at the irreparable loss which they and that country have sustained; — Therefore,

Resolved, That the services of Daniel Webster to his country demand, from the members of this Bar, an expression of their deep sorrow at his decease, and of their admiration for the unrivalled greatness of his character.

Resolved, That this Bar desire to withdraw for a season from their ordinary pursuits, to meditate upon the loss of the most eminent of their number, and to mingle their sorrows with those of a nation that now mourns his departure.

Resolved, That we deeply sympathize with the family of our deceased Brother, and that a copy of these Resolutions, as an expression of that sympathy, be transmitted to them.

Resolved, That the Attorney-General of the Commonwealth be requested to present these Resolutions to the Supreme Judicial Court now in session, and ask that they may be entered on their records.

Upon presenting the foregoing resolutions, Attorney-General CLIFFORD addressed the Court:

May it please your Honors — At the request of my Brethren of the Bar of the Old Colony, and as their organ, I rise to ask your Honors to suspend for a while our customary labors, in recognition of an event, which requires, from us to you, no formal announcement. It has already shrouded the nation in gloom, and bowed in grief the universal heart.

Our elder Brother of the Bar, our professional exemplar, guide, and friend, Daniel Webster, is no more! And where, throughout the broad land, which is filled with the tokens of his labors and his life, where can the homelike feeling of personal grief, for a personal loss, find a more natural and fitting expression, than among his professional brethren of the Old Colony? Here was the latest home of his affections. It will be the last home of all of him that belongs to earth.

At our first annual assembling in the presence of this Court, where his living voice has so often uttered the highest wisdom, and where his spirit will long linger, I am desired to submit to the Court certain resolutions, which the Bar have adopted, as an expression of their sense of the magnitude of the loss which they, in common with the whole country, have sustained. They have had no time, or opportunity, nor have they desired it, to clothe in any elaborate forms of rhetoric, the sentiments with which this solemn event has filled their hearts. They offer these brief resolutions as a simple and spontaneous expression of the feeling which this great national bereavement has inspired. And I shall most satisfactorily discharge the duty with which I am charged by my brethren, and best answer their expectations and wishes, by accompanying them with a few simple prefatory words.

Under this autumn sun, a rich harvest has been gathered into the garner of mortality. In both hemispheres, the two foremost men of the two leading nations of the civilized world, to each of whom was committed by their Creator the perilous gift of the ten talents, have been summoned by Him to give an account of their stewardship; the soldier-statesman — the lawyer-statesman, — each in his sphere mightiest among the mighty; both, too, following close upon the footsteps of another great luminary of our profession, whose mortal light has just faded behind yonder western hills, and for whose departure the tears are yet moist upon a nation's cheek.

Were it not, Mr. Chief Justice, for our Christian faith in that overruling Providence, whose dread summons it is that has just been so often sounded in our ears, and who we know "ordereth all things well," as he "doeth his pleasure among the inhabitants of the earth," we might be tempted, in this hour of our bereavement, to utter the desponding lamentation which the great poet has so touchingly expressed in verse.

> We have fallen upon evil days,
> Star after star decays,
> The brightest names, that shed
> Light o'er the land, have fled.

In contemplating the character and career of Mr. Webster as a lawyer, we can scarcely measure the magnitude of the debt which, as lawyers, we owe to him. Let those who aspire to reach the pure heights of this noble profession — and who that is stirred by a spark of worthy ambition, does not so aspire? — remember the encouragement his life has furnished to every youth whose days are devoted to its toilsome pursuit. What a reflected light have his great achievements thrown back upon the humble home of his childhood among the New Hampshire hills; from which, by patient and unremitting labor, devoted with unsurpassed fidelity to his profession, he advanced to a position in the world's regard which will make that humble home a shrine of pilgrimage through all coming time. Wherever, throughout the world, justice is administered among men, he has made the name of an American lawyer an honored name. His worthy conceptions of the true character of the profession, the exalted aims which he early set before himself, in its pursuit, and the admirable and resolute training of all his great faculties to meet its requirements, enabled him to shed upon it a new glory, by showing to the world its fitness for training the intellectual powers for the highest achievements of statesmanship. To the most brilliant effort of his public career, he carried the training and discipline of the lawyer's mind, and through it he achieved a triumph for himself and for his country, the effects of which will last as long as the Union which it established, and the memory of which will be coeval with the knowledge of his native tongue.

When he was summoned to that "Great Debate," he found that in certain portions of the country there was a prevalent, confused idea, that the Government of the United States was a mere confederation, or congeries of independent States, a phantom, an unreal mockery of power. With a masterly exertion of that great faculty which he possessed in so eminent a degree beyond all other men, of making the most complicated and difficult problem simple and intelligible to the humblest mind, he established that Government on the irreversible convictions of the people of this country, as a real, living, substantial thing — the efficient Government of a great Empire, founded upon the sovereignty of the whole people.

No other man of our time could have accomplished this great work, so vital to every interest of this Union. Mighty in intellect, of a most majestic presence, of infinite gifts and resources, the impress of greatness was stamped upon him by the hand of the Almighty. He seemed to be the very type and embodiment of Shakspeare's apostrophe to man: "How noble in reason — how infinite in faculties — in form and moving, how express and admirable — in apprehension how like a God!"

But he has gone from amongst us, and we would turn in cheerful Christian faith from the gloomy aspect of this great bereavement, to the felicities which attended the close of his earthly career.

He had rounded the full measure of threescore years and ten. The great record of his long life's services to his country had been made up. His work was finished. He enjoyed the full fruition of that Eastern benediction which is so dear to the heart of man, that it has been wrought into the expression of a universal wish, "May you die among your kindred." More than all, it was vouchsafed to him to realize the hope, which he once expressed in language of surpassing sublimity and fervor, that "When his eye should be turned for the last time to behold the sun in heaven, he might not see him shining on the broken and dishonored fragments of a once glorious Union." Thanks be to God, "its last feeble and lingering glance beheld the gorgeous ensign of the Republic, known and honored throughout the earth, still full high advanced — not a stripe erased or polluted, or a star obscured."

And thus this great man departed. Surrounded by all

> — that which should accompany old age,
> As honor, love, obedience, troops of friends.

His last words still echo in our ears, as they will echo in the ears of other generations of men, long after we shall have passed away like the dust of the summer threshing-floor. "I still live." How true for him, in this world, throughout all time. "*Vita brevis est; cursus gloriæ sempiternus.*" May we not humbly trust that it was equally true for him in that higher and better sense which assures us of his participation in the gracious promise, — "He that liveth and believeth in me, shall never die."

Mr. Clifford then read the resolutions adopted by the Bar, and moved the Court that they be entered upon its records, and that the Court do now adjourn.

Chief Justice SHAW responded on the part of the Court as follows:

Gentlemen of the Old Colony Bar — This Court, in behalf of whom I now speak, do most cordially assure you of their full participation in the feelings of profound sadness and grief, which everywhere pervade this great community, in view of the signal bereavement which we all deplore, and their sincere sympathy in the sentiments expressed in the resolutions which you have now offered. We are called upon to lament the loss of an illustrious man, of an eminent statesman, of a profound jurist, and eloquent advocate. It seems fitting, therefore, amidst the exciting interests, the exacting cares, and the laborious duties, to which we are devoted, to pause, and listen with reverent awe, to the deep lessons of wisdom, which Providence is teaching us, by an event so impressive. We are thus forcibly reminded, that however illustrious any man may become for learning and wisdom, that however important and necessary his life and services may seem to his friends, his country, and his race, to whatever height of fame and prosperity he may have reached, still the time of his departure comes as it comes to all, when all the attractions of earth lose their lustre and their force, and we are awakened to a deep conviction of the solemn realities of another life, in comparison with which all the interests of this our mortal being, seem trifling and insignificant.

We are now forcibly reminded by all that we see and feel, that a great man has fallen among us. Mr. Webster has long been in the full view of our whole community, regarded as a man of great wisdom, a prudent guide and counsellor, who had the best good of his country and of his race always at heart. Conspicuous alike for his commanding talents, his large and comprehensive views, the purity and correctness of all his great purposes, he was looked to, as one who could be safely trusted in the darkest hours of his country's prospects, to protect her from suffering and peril, from within and from without. Mr. Webster's whole course of public life, in which he has been steadily advancing in honor and usefulness, has been known and visible to the whole community; and the strong and universal manifestation of grief and sadness, which have everywhere followed the news of his decease, afford ample proof of the firm hold which he had upon the confidence and affections of the people.

As a statesman, he was equally distinguished by the resources of his capacious mind, and the eminent wisdom of his counsels. In the exertion of his great powers, in public affairs, no partial or sectional interests, no private or party views could allure him from the path of the general and public good. Dazzled by no visionary theories, deluded by no speculative projects, his views were decidedly practical and attainable; looking to the actual and various conditions, to all the liberal and industrial pursuits of the whole people of the Union, he was equally comprehensive in his regards, and just and discriminating in his measures. He was ardently devoted to the support of the Constitution in its integrity, because he regarded it, under Providence, as the only safeguard and guaranty of the Union; and he loved the Union, because, in his sober judgment, its preservation is essentially necessary to the peace, liberty, and security, and consequently to the best and truest interests of the whole community. Peace, internal harmony, security for all personal, social, and political rights, these, if we may judge from his clear and often repeated declarations, were, in his view, the leading object of all government; and that, practically, that government is best which gives the highest encouragement to personal exertion, and the largest scope to individual enterprise, in every honest and laudable pursuit, which can be given, consistently with a just regard and an effectual security to the equal rights of all.

But this is not the time or place to attempt a discriminating or detailed view of Mr. Webster's high qualities as a statesman. He will long be remembered throughout the Union, on the ocean and in the workshop, on the farm, and in every walk of industry, as the defender of the Constitution, the faithful friend of the Union, and the advocate of the just rights of all the members of this great and growing community.

In addressing myself to a body devoted to the study and practice of the law, and the administration of justice, many of whom have been associated with him as a professional brother and friend, and all of whom have been accustomed to regard him as an honor to the profession which they love, it seems more fitting to allude briefly to the character of Mr. Webster, as a jurist and an advocate. He early selected the study of the law, which, when faithfully and honorably pursued, may justly be regarded as a high and honorable profession, inasmuch as it looks to the practical assertion of right, liberty, and justice, as its leading object. He soon distinguished himself for great research, for large and comprehensive views of the law, and of those broad principles of right and justice, having their deep and immovable foundations in the moral laws of our nature, which constitute the true basis of all law. As soon as he entered on the career of practice, he became distinguished at once, as a learned jurist and an eloquent advocate. With a natural acumen and power of legal discrimination quite unsurpassed, with a force of logic and power of eloquence, which gave to every argument its most efficient impress, he soon attained to a rank in his profession, which elevated him to an equality with those who had been previously regarded as the lights of the professional firmament in this and the neighboring States, and who were then held in the highest estimation for professional eminence.

In one department, that of Constitutional law, he was peculiarly distinguished, and gained a reputation second perhaps to no one, unless that of him who was so long distinguished as the head of the first judicial tribunal of the country.

Starting, like other students, with no extraordinary external aid, and reaching the highest eminence, the example of Mr. Webster may well be held up as an encouragement to young men, struggling in the earlier stages of a profession requiring persevering effort and untiring industry. Let those who have watched the dawn of his early professional reputation, the splendor of his meridian success, and have now witnessed its brilliant close, take courage, and hope on, holding his virtues and his industry as a high example, and his renown as a never-failing encouragement to patience and perseverance in well doing.

In these remarks, brief and hasty as they are, I would not wholly overlook the example and influence of Mr. Webster, as a man, a friend, a member of society, and a public benefactor. Always foremost in the promotion of all social institutions, for education, for the improvement of mind, for the cultivation of the social affections, for the improvement of taste, he did much to give value and dignity, as well as grace and elegance to refined society. Devoted to the cultivation of letters, seeking in the annals of the past the examples of the wise and good for the encouragement and improvement of the present times, venerating especially the virtues and achievements of our hardy ancestors, he was ever ready, with his treasures of learning and his powers of eloquence, to unite with others in commemoration of great events, and interesting epochs. Wherever particular times and places have been consecrated to the love of liberty and of country, to the commemoration of illustrious public benefactors, there was he prepared to utter the eloquent words of wisdom to listening crowds, where their import would be most impressive. At Plymouth Rock, at Bunker Hill, at the Monument of Washington, wherever the wise and good assembled to commune and learn wisdom from the past, his presence, and his glowing eloquence, were not wanting.

But he is gone; a great light and glory of our age has departed from our sight, not indeed until he had done all that a great statesman, an illustrious advocate, a humble and devout Christian, a most distinguished citizen and man could do, to improve and benefit his age and his race, and especially, as his crowning excellence, to turn their hearts and thoughts from the alluring engagements and engrossing cares of this transitory life, to a higher and more enduring state of existence beyond the grave. In this view, it is fit that we now regard him as one who has done much to benefit one world, without omitting the higher function of pointing the way to another. Let us be grateful to a benign Providence for all the good which the statesman and benefactor was able to do; and let us profit by the good examples he has given us, and the grave lessons which his life, character, and death have taught us. Whilst devoting ourselves faithfully, and with all our powers, to the discharge of our duties, those duties which we fondly flatter ourselves are high and important, and which do indeed touch the dearest earthly interests of men, and of communities, let us never forget, that amidst these, as part of these, and necessary to their just performance, that there is one duty never to be overlooked, that of a steady and constant regard, and of a frequent and solemn reflection on the higher subjects of life, death, and immortality; that, whether we live or die, we may be found in the way of duty.

PROCEEDINGS

OF THE

BOSTON SCHOOL COMMITTEE.

18

PROCEEDINGS OF THE BOSTON SCHOOL COMMITTEE.

At the meeting of the Boston Grammar School Committee, on Tuesday, November 22, the following resolutions were submitted by Dr. Adams:

Whereas, Almighty God has seen fit to remove from us, by death, one whom all unite in calling "the foremost man of our country," the School Committee of the city of Boston, at their first meeting, after the announcement of this sad intelligence, not only would avail themselves of the opportunity, but deem it their duty, to give utterance to their feelings on this solemn occasion; Therefore,

Resolved, That while we submit with all humility to this afflicting dispensation, we cannot but deplore for our country and the world, this extinction of their brightest ornament and ablest mind.

Resolved, That in the death of Daniel Webster we recognize the loss of one in whom existed that rare combination of the brightest intellect and the largest capacity, under the government and control of moral influences; one, in whose own language, our common school system was called "that celestial and that earthly light," under which the young men of our country shall come up, fitted intellectually and morally to sustain and perpetuate our free institutions.

Resolved, That while the deep, mellow tones of that voice, which have so often delighted our ears, shall be heard no more forever, and the significant glance of those once piercing eyes, are now dimmed in death; yet in his own last words, "He still lives;" yes, and will live by his teachings and noble example in the mind and heart of every true American, so long as the last glimmer of the light of human freedom shall continue "to linger and play on the summit" of our temple of liberty.

Rev. HUBBARD WINSLOW said:

Mr. President — I rise to second, most cordially, the resolutions just offered. I do not propose to occupy much time with remarks; but before engaging in our customary business, at this first meeting of the board since the death of Mr. Webster, it becomes us to pause and consecrate our first thoughts to that great and solemn event.

The mournful tidings have, ere this, gone over the length and breadth of the land; the entire nation is now in tears. And they are neither feigned nor ordinary tears. They come from the deepest fountain of the soul, and they refuse to be dried up. The more the heart seeks to be comforted, the more it refuses all comfort, but such as comes only from above.

In a beautiful German fable, representing our progenitor as weeping over the first human victim of death, and exclaiming, "What now remains for me, in my lamentation?" a bright cherub from the skies answers, "Der Blick gen Himmel!" A look to Heaven! That only remains to us — to this mourning nation; in the loss of its truest friend and brightest ornament. That same cherub still hovers on poised wing, between earth and heaven; still he beckons us, and points the eye of hope to those golden portals — those everlasting gates — through which the immortal spirit of the great man has just passed, into regions of uncreated light and glory. From those imperial heights, beyond the reach of mortality and change, a voice came to us from him, "not dead, but gone before,"

"I still live." This, sir, is our consolation. Webster still lives, and will live forever.

We should not be willing to accept the benefits which he has bestowed upon us, great as they are, if they must needs cost the final sacrifice of him by whom they have been bestowed. But when we think of him as still living, looking down from the skies upon us, and contemplating the future glories of this and other nations, as enhanced by his labors and his undying principles, our hearts are comforted, and we gratefully accept the priceless legacy he has bequeathed us.

And what a legacy! "The great principles of Magna Charta, of the English Revolution, and especially of the American Revolution, of the English language." Well might he say — "The day-spring from on high has visited us; the country has been called back to conscience and to duty. There is no longer imminent danger of dissolution in these United States. We shall live, and not die. We shall live as united Americans; and those who have supposed they could sever us, that they could rend one American heart from another, and that speculation and hypothesis, that secession and metaphysics could tear us asunder, will find themselves wofully mistaken."

To eulogize Daniel Webster is no part of my object. It as far transcends my power as it does his necessity. Those of us who have known him more than a quarter of a century, in the various walks of public and of private life, have his eulogy already deeply written on our hearts.

That noble and majestic form, that colossal and

classic head, those large and brilliant eyes; that countenance, so benignant in smile and so terrible in frown; the *tout ensemble* of that entire personage, so peculiar, so striking, so superior to that of any other human being we have ever seen, must forever retain a place in our most vivid conceptions. Viewing him merely in his personal appearance, "we ne'er shall see his like again." But in his mental being, he is far more unlike all others. There is in it a combination of grandeur and simplicity, of greatness and minuteness, of strength and delicacy, which were never before so perfectly blended in a human mind. His intellect was as the ocean, which he so much loved, and which only seemed large enough for him, on which, in fair weather, the lightest skiff can float safely, and in which the most deeply freighted ships of merchandise find no bottom. The child could understand him and be instructed by what he said, while the most profound thinker saw in him a "vasty deep," which he could not fathom.

When we contemplate him in the forum, carrying judge and jury, and all others, with him, by argument, at once so simple that a child could comprehend it, and so mighty that the loftiest intellect bowed reverently to it; when we think of him on those public occasions, when mighty themes of general interest inspired his great heart, and poured from his lips in strains of surpassing pathos, sublimity, and classic beauty, to the outbursting admiration of assembled thousands; when he is present to our minds, as he ever will be, in the lustrous character of expounder and defender of the American Constitution, unfolding and impressing its sacred lessons of eternal obligations, and thus cementing the bonds of the National Union; when we regard him as the civilian, the diplomatist, the statesman, defining rights and duties, establishing laws of reciprocity, and settling great principles, to be henceforth recognized by all civilized communities and nations, and doing all with a depth and reach of wisdom that never failed; when we behold him fighting the nation's battles, securing its victories, protecting its rights and its honors, unfurling its triumphant stripes and stars over all seas, by the mere power of his intellect, and without shedding a drop of the people's blood, or wasting an ounce of their treasure; and then, when, from the high seats of official eminence, we follow him to the farm, the neighborhood, the fireside, and ponder those tender graces of affection which made him so dear to his family, servants, workmen, neighbors, and all who knew him, — which allowed no creature, human or animal, to suffer, when he could afford relief, — and which seemed to inspire the very cattle upon his grounds with a sentiment of admiration and love for their owner; and when, especially, we see him as a Christian, bowing his great mind, with the simplicity of a child, to the teachings of Jesus Christ, surrendering himself cordially to that faith which looks for honor, glory, and immortality in Heaven, and resigning all that was mortal in a way that made death an apotheosis rather than a dissolution; — I say, as he rises before us, in all these various aspects and relations, we are constrained to acknowledge that he was a man by himself, and that to have been privileged to live in the same age, the same country, the same community with him, imposes on us a debt of no ordinary gratitude. Henceforth, the age, and the country that gave him birth, will be illustrious in the annals of time.

But, Sir, it was with another view that I rose to speak. We meet here as the friends and guardians of education. To us are intrusted, especially, the interests of our common and our public schools. It was the common school system to which we are here officially devoted, and which is the crowning glory of this country, that gave Daniel Webster to this world. But for this, that gigantic intellect had slumbered, unknowing and unknown, with those granite rocks that gave him birth. It is this system of common schools spreading over the land, all-searching and pervading, that develops the hidden treasures of the mind, and often from the most obscure retreats calls forth to life and power those mighty intellects which become the ornament of letters, the pride of science, the defence of religion, and the pillars of State.

And, Sir, the debt which that great man owed to the school system of this country, he has richly paid. The man never lived who thought more highly of their importance, and did more to inspirit and enrich them. As a friend of his was once riding with him through his native State, and was speaking of the dangers and prospects of our country, "There," said Mr. Webster, pointing to an humble school-house, and to a small church near it, "is the foundation of all our hopes, both for the present and the future. It is to the religion and the schools which our fathers planted, that our Republic owes its existence; without them there can be no rational liberty. So long as these are fostered, our institutions are safe; whenever they shall be neglected, the knell of republicanism will be tolled."

Such sentiments were perpetually beaming out in all his private conversations and public speeches in reference to the destinies of our nation. "I have seen," said he, "and others of my age have seen, the church and the school-house rise and stand in the very centre of the forest, and seen them resorted to in the midst of winter snows. And when these things lie at the foundation and commencement of society; where the worship of God, the observance of morals, and the culture of the human mind, are springs of action with those who take hold of the original forest, to subdue it by strong arms and strong muscles, there, depend upon it, the people never fail. Everywhere, *everywhere*, on her hills and rivers, are these school-houses. The school-house; who shall speak of that throughout New England, as it ought to be spoken of? Who shall speak, in proper language, of the wisdom, and foresight, and benevolence, and sagacity of our forefathers, in establishing a general system of public instruction as a great public police for the benefit of the whole, as a business in which all are interested! The world had previously seen nothing like it, although some parts of the world have since copied from it."

Henceforth, sir, that great man will be intimately associated with the educational systems of our country. The Bar, the Forum, the Senate, the Council-

Chamber, shall not exclusively claim it; it shall be known, and honored, and loved, from sea to sea, by all the friends of education, as the name of the most illustrious champion of their cause. Henceforth, all who toil in the arduous work of education shall know that the blessing of Daniel Webster is upon them. They are engaging in the very work which he believed to be, before all others, essential to our welfare as individuals, and to our safety as a nation. It was not merely the college, the higher halls of science, that he, by his matchless eloquence, defended; the common school, even the infant school, engaged his attention and his heart, and called forth his most impassioned commendation. His standing motto was, *Solem e mundo tollunt, qui scientiam e vita tollunt.*

But, sir, he has done more than merely to commend our school system; he has himself engaged, personally, in the work of teaching, and has pronounced the time thus spent the most profitable portion of his life. We have thus not only his counsel to guide, but his example to inspirit us.

Nor is this all; — it is, indeed, the least part. He has poured the measureless wealth of his own intellect into all the schools and colleges of the land. There is scarcely a child in America, twelve years old, whose mind has not been enriched by his speeches and orations. Those chaste and massive sentences, those simple and resistless arguments, those bold and brilliant flashes of imagination, those notes of thundering, subduing, awful eloquence, those impassioned appeals to patriotism, have found their way to every school-boy's heart, and have begun to mould the mental character of the rising race.

Hence the enthusiasm which all our youth feel in regard to Daniel Webster. They know little, and care less, for party politics. They have not yet entered the arena of political strife; but they have caught the fire of that mighty spirit's eloquence, they feel the benign influence of a lofty mind working upon theirs; and the same magic impulse which prompts them to rise higher in mental excellence, prompts them to do honor to their great master.

Their minds have become so much moulded and inspired by his, that they instinctively love and honor him. His speeches are destined to do more, in my opinion, to promote the great objects of education, to form correct habits of thinking and speaking, and to put the rising American race in possession of a chastened, eloquent, powerful literature, than any other instrumentality of the nineteenth century.

But, sir, I did not intend to say so much. My only apology is, that I could not say less. While we pause to meditate upon our irreparable loss, let us not forget that we have other and higher duties, and duties which time will not wait for us to perform.

> Omnes eodem cogimur; omnium
> Versatur urna, serius ocyus
> Sors exitura, et nos æternum
> Exilium impositura cymbæ.

No, sir; it is not to eternal exile, as the heathen poet says, that we are destined. If faithful to those higher duties, we may look, in the light of Christian faith, to that same celestial home of eternal friendship and glory, into which our illustrious friend has entered before us. The dying scene of that immortal man! Who of us does not wish that his last end may be like his? Socrates died like a philosopher; Webster, like a Christian. His death was the crowning glory of a glorious life. He wanted no Charon's boat to float him over the dark wave to the land of eternal exile; — a convoy of shining angels were in attendance; and as his calm, piercing gaze shot up the long bright track in which they were to conduct him, he exclaimed, amid his last distinct utterances on earth: — "*This day I shall be in life, in glory, in blessedness.*" Let us, then, with such examples before us, gird up our minds to duty, and be faithful to our high mission.

Mr. Stevenson addressed the Board as follows:

I concur with the gentleman who has just spoken, as to the propriety of the action which is proposed, and do not doubt that every member of the Board will concur with him.

We are members of a sorrow-stricken community. It is no ordinary public grief which has so taken possession of the minds of men; but each feels as he would feel if a valuable member of his own household had been taken away from his sight forever. The very depths of feeling have been sounded. Ever since the event which we mourn, a political Sabbath has prevailed. The all-pervading feeling is taking every proper form of expression. Perhaps no more impressive scene was ever witnessed than that which exhibited itself in Faneuil Hall on Wednesday last. Grief had called together a multitude of men. The first time that that hall had ever been shrouded in the drapery of mourning, he himself had stood there to speak of those over whom had passed that mysterious change which separates the mortal from the immortal; and then the fact that all that was mortal of himself was at rest, while his majestic spirit was in the presence of Almighty God, had filled the same place.

The beautiful eloquence of gifted orators could move that audience only to tears; and thousands of strong men stood there and wept.

The echoes of the temple, which had been accustomed to be awakened into a tumult at the bare whisper of his name, slept in the silence of sadness. It could not but be so. For all realized what a voice was left when his place on earth was unoccupied, and all knew that, in many respects, that place must remain unoccupied.

For how true it is, that there is not with us, or of us, any other man, for whose judgment all — all can look, as they have been accustomed to look for his, whenever there has presented itself any new question affecting the interests, or the honor, or the peace, or the progress of this great nation. Whether we had realized it before or not, we now felt how we had looked for and waited for that judgment.

Now, when we need his counsels, as we shall, they will no longer be given to us in the living words, that have burnt their influences into our very convictions, but we must look for them in the storehouses of our memories, and in the recorded pages of his wisdom. He has gone from the midst of us, but not without having performed the full mission of a man.

The teacher rests from his labors. The results of

those labors are an invaluable legacy to each of us. How true it is that he who would comprehend the philosophy of, or even appreciate the full value of, the institutions under which this people have been trying the experiment of self-government, must read and study his expositions of them, or the lesson will not be learned. Read his works, and feel what a blessing civil and religious liberty is. Read them, and feel what a blessing it is to live under a government of laws rather than under a government of men. Read them; and if, which God forbid, the obligations of the Constitution of your country hang loosely on you, rivet them with his thoughts.

The form which we loved to meet has gone from us forever. Gratitude will provide a monument. It will not be so imperishable as his thoughts; it will not be so enduring as the lessons he has taught; but it will be a shrine, before which we and our children, and our children's children may bow, as before an altar, to civil and religious freedom.

May we profit by the example which he has left to us, of a firm faith, a deep devotion, an unfaltering trust, a pure love towards the Father of his spirit. We will make an application, other than that which he probably intended, still a truthful one, of the last words which fell from his mortal lips, so soon to be sealed by the angel,—"I still live." That assurance was not obliterated when that seal was fixed. His spirit is God's. His fame is ours. His works will praise him; our words cannot.

Mr. Derby followed, and said:

Mr. President — I rise to sustain these resolutions. I cannot hope to add force to what has been so eloquently said by the gentleman who preceded me, but a high functionary of the Union has died — the most distinguished citizen of our State has breathed his last — our City Councils have given public expression to their griefs, and I feel it to be our duty to pass these resolutions and adjourn.

It has been my privilege to know Mr. Webster from childhood. I knew him when at school in New Hampshire. I subsequently studied three years in his office, and I have cherished his acquaintance until his death. I can bear testimony to the giant grasp of his intellect, for I have often witnessed its exertion. I can speak of his herculean powers, not from report alone, but from personal experience, for I have lived to meet him in the forum, and have four times felt the weight and almost resistless powers of his arguments. Let me add my humble testimony to the colossal greatness of his intellect.

There are, however, traits of character deeply impressed on my memory, for which I reverence him as much as for his intellect. Amid the strife of the forum he preserved the freshness of his feelings and reflections. Some men, in their devotion to one great idea, become callous to those affections, but it was not so with Mr. Webster. I can remember well the loss of his partner, Mr. Bliss. He died in the prime of life, and in the flush of success. I recall the intense solicitude of Mr. Webster; how he paced his office all day in silence, absorbed in grief, while we looked for the melancholy event. Nor shall I ever forget his devotion to his first wife, when arrested by sickness at New York. Mr. Webster had achieved a name in the Supreme Court. He was retained in nearly all the important cases at Washington. The Court was about to open, fortune and honor were before him. He gave up his retainers, he sacrificed his prospects for years. Wealth and advancement had no attractions to draw him from the couch of his wife; he lingered there for months to receive the last sigh of the partner of his bosom.

We meet in this hall, however, as the guardians of education; let us cherish the remembrance that he has, in his addresses, rendered service to the cause. He has ever pointed to the school-house as the ark of our safety. His giant efforts are embalmed in our school-books, enshrined with the speeches of Demosthenes and Cicero, Burke, Sheridan, and Chatham, to animate and inspire the youth of our country.

He was himself a bright exemplar of the power of education. Let us trace him from his humble home in the wilds of New Hampshire; let us imagine him standing beside his father, and recall his interview in the field, with a member of Congress, and the words of that noble father when he said, "that man is in Congress because he had an education, and I might have filled his place could I have had the benefit of a school. You shall be educated." Let us follow him from the labors of the farm and the menial offices of the inn, to the humble school of Master Tappan, to the fireside of the village clergyman, to Exeter and to Dartmouth. Let us observe him enter the bleak school-house, through the snow of a New Hampshire winter, with his breath freezing upon his collar, to aid the humble means of his parent by his ill-paid labors as a teacher. Let us follow him to the Academy, where he teaches by day and copies deeds by night, while he educates his brother, and strives to study his profession. Let us view him in the Short Street School, rousing the genius of Everett. Let us accompany him to the triumphs of the Bar and the Senate, until we leave him Secretary of State. Education has lifted him from the dust; from turning the sods of the valley, to guide the destinies of nations, to exert a mighty influence over the civilized world. Is not his whole career illustrative of the power of education? Is it not a noble incentive to the master in his humble toils, to the ambitious youth struggling with adversity? And does it not attest the importance of that system of schools which we meet here to promote, a system so rapidly diffusing itself over the Union? Should every million we invest, produce but one Webster, would it not be well invested?

The old ballad of Chevy Chase recites that, when the King of Scotland was told of the death of Douglas, he replied that he had no warriors left like him; although the King of England, when mourning for his Percy's death, could replace him with fifty more. Like Scotland's King, we mourn our Douglas dead; more than England's King, we now mourn our matchless Percy; but the system of education which has given us one Webster, will eventually give us more. There is a wide domain of talent to be cultivated; rich material is in store for us. It shall not be wasted.

Through the dim vista of the future, I see, under the electric power of education, other Websters rise from their obscurity to guide the councils, and mould the destinies of our nation.

> Full many a gem of purest ray serene,
> The dark unfathomed caves of ocean bear.

The cavern must be explored. The precious stones must be extracted and sent forth, radiant and sparkling, to adorn the high places of the nation. In honoring Webster, we show our respect for education. We do but participate also in the grief of a nation. The solemn bell has tolled his requiem from spire to spire, city to city, until its murmurs are lost in the surges of the Pacific.

His loss has been deplored by eloquent voices still ringing from thousands of pulpits.

The thunder of cannon has proclaimed the nation's grief from shore to shore, fit memento of him whose lightning has flashed in the Senate Chamber, and whose thunder has rolled in the Forum.

Even nature, in her sombre aspect, seems to mourn his loss. The groves of Franklin and of Marshfield sigh at his departure; and may we not apply to the orator and lover of nature, as well as to the poet, those beautiful lines of Scott —

> Call it not vain, they do not err,
> Who say, that when the Poet dies,
> Mute Nature mourns her worshipper,
> And celebrates his obsequies;
> Who say tall cliff, and cavern lone,
> For the departed Bard make moan;
> That mountains weep in crystal rill;

That flowers in tears of balm distil;
Through his loved groves, that breezes sigh,
And oaks, in deeper groan, reply;
And Ocean tells its rushing wave
To murmur dirges round his grave.

The resolutions were passed by a unanimous vote.

PROCEEDINGS AND RESOLUTIONS

OF

VARIOUS ASSOCIATIONS.

PROCEEDINGS OF THE WEBSTER EXECUTIVE COMMITTEE.

A MEETING of the Webster Executive Committee was held on Monday evening, October 25, General J. S. Tyler in the chair. Some discussion was had as to the course of duty devolved upon the Club by the death of Mr. Webster, and a committee of seven persons was raised to consider the subject and report resolutions.

At an adjourned meeting on Tuesday evening, October 26, Mr. WINSLOW, from the Committee of seven appointed on Monday evening, submitted the following resolutions:

Resolved, That while overwhelmed with grief by the death of our illustrious statesman and patriot, we would yet bow submissively to the will of Him who does all things well.

Resolved, That our sorrow is mingled with deep and earnest gratitude that Daniel Webster was given to this nation, and that his life and teachings have impressed upon it lessons of lofty wisdom and patriotism, which will not be forgotten.

Resolved, That as his bereaved companion and other family relatives mourn not alone, but the whole nation mourns with them, it is our fervent prayer that they may ever receive the sustaining sympathies and benedictions of all the people of the land, as the only return which can now be offered for a debt of gratitude that can never be paid.

Resolved, That as a mark of respect for the great man, whose death we mourn, this convention recommend to the friends of the deceased to wear a badge of crape on the left arm for thirty days.

Resolved, That as some special tribute is due from us to those great national principles maintained and defended by Mr. Webster while he lived, and dear to him in death, in addition to uniting most cordially in all the civic honors paid to him, we will also unite in a celebration that shall distinctly recognize and set forth those principles, in an eulogy to be delivered by an orator of our own selection, and that we invite our friends in all parts of the Commonwealth to join with us in said celebration.

Resolved, That ——— be a committee to make all necessary arrangements to carry the above resolutions into effect; to select the orator, appoint the time and place, and report to the Executive Committee at an early day.

The resolutions were adopted, and Messrs. C. A. White, C. Torrey, and T. Wiley were appointed as the Committee called for in the last resolve.

PROCEEDINGS OF THE WHIG WARD AND COUNTY CONVENTION.

A MEETING of the Whig Ward and County Convention was held on the evening of October 29, and a series of appropriate resolutions were adopted. FARNHAM PLUMMER, Esq., in introducing the resolutions, spoke as follows:

Some five days have elapsed since those startling minute-guns, booming forth upon a bright and calm Sabbath morning, announced to the citizens of Boston and its vicinity the painful fact that the great heart of that eminent statesman and illustrious fellow-citizen, Daniel Webster, had forever ceased its pulsations. The interval has been occupied by the readiest writers and the ablest speakers, and our language has been found inadequate to express the deep feeling and emotion which are felt not only by the people of Boston, but also by the whole nation. The Committee have, therefore, approached the subject with great diffidence. They have embodied a few facts in simple words, and have only to add a hope that they may be unanimously adopted.

Resolved, That this Convention has heard with deep and poignant grief of the decease of our illustrious fellow-citizen, the Honorable Daniel Webster, and that, remembering his services as Representative of this city in Congress — as a Senator of our beloved Commonwealth in the Senate of the United States, and as on two occasions Secretary of State of the United States — we feel the truth so beautifully expressed by President Fillmore, that his fame belongs to America, and the admiration of it to all mankind.

Resolved, That as members of the Whig party, — of which he was through life the ablest representative, and in the advancement of whose doctrines and policy he made some of his noblest efforts, — we feel the irreparable loss our country has sustained; — but that, above and beyond all party considerations, as American citizens, as constituent parts of this great and glorious Union, we recall with pride his patriotism, bounded by no State lines, knowing no North, no South, no East, no West; — his care, his solicitude, and his unremitting labor for the perpetuation and aggrandizement of our common country, and for the preservation of that Constitution under whose blessings, by the aid of a kind Providence, we hope ourselves and our posterity may live — a great, a happy, and above all a *united* people.

Resolved, That while his long and varied life has been but one series of victories achieved and triumphs gained for his State, his Country, and for Constitutional Liberty everywhere, we can but feel, as friends of the Christian Religion, that nothing was wanting to the perfection of such a life, but such an ending of it; and that the brilliancy of his career is and could be equalled only by the splendor and beauty of its close.

Resolved, That a copy of these resolutions, signed by the President and Secretary of this Convention, be transmitted to the family of Mr. Webster, in token of our respect for his name, and of our condolence in this season of their affliction.

PROCEEDINGS OF GRANITE CLUB, NO. 1.

On Monday evening, October 25, a special meeting of the Granite club, No. 1, was held. The attendance was very large. Vice-President Orcutt, of Chelsea, presided. The meeting was called for the purpose of making some demonstration of respect to the memory of Daniel Webster. Hon. Aaron Hobart, in a few able and appropriate remarks, offered the following resolutions:

Resolved, That there are occasions, when, without surrendering principles or intermitting duties, it is becoming, even in the midst of a great canvass for political power in the nation, to forget that we are partisans, and remember only that all are citizens of one common country.

Resolved, That on no occasion has this reflection become so impressive as by the death of Daniel Webster; of whom it can be said with emphatic truth, that if he belonged to any party or to any part of the Union, while living, his memory and his history belong to his country, to the whole Union, and to the world.

Resolved, That the democratic party, forgetting wherein they differed, will ever hold in grateful remembrance that great quality of the great mind of Daniel Webster, which led him, in almost every national crisis, to adhere to the Union with a patriotism that could not be bounded by party limits, and with a devotion to that Union equalled only by the eloquence with which he enforced its binding obligations upon all sections of the country; that they will look for no spots on the sun of his glorious fame, while they can see shining there to light posterity his manly vindication of popular government and independence in Greece, South America, and Hungary, against the dogmas of the "Holy Allies" and despots of Europe, his early development of the great democratic principles of free trade and solid currency, and his noble championship of the Constitution in 1830 and 1850, for the supremacy of the laws and the integrity of the Union.

Resolved, That in the great lights in which he will be viewed hereafter, he will be regarded by all men, who honor genius and intellect, and noble thoughts and manly acts, as a splendid model of the character developed under our Republican institutions, and an illustrious instance of the power of character thus developed, to defend that Union upon which depend all Republican institutions on this Continent, and all hope of their organization in any other portion of the globe.

Resolved, That the last words of the dying statesman, "*I still live,*" spoke not only of that immortality beyond earth, in which he held a confiding faith, but will forever be true and full of meaning among men; for while the Union lives, it will be said of him, as he himself said of the illustrious dead, JEFFERSON and ADAMS, when pronouncing their eulogy in Faneuil Hall, "His body is buried in peace, but his name liveth evermore."

Resolved, That it is honorable to human nature to find, on occasions of the decease of eminent statesmen, the concurrence of all political parties in doing honor to their memories; and in this spirit, and with full hearts, we lay our offerings of profound grief, respect, and admiration upon the tomb of Daniel Webster; rejoicing, nevertheless, that in answer to his own fervent prayer of patriotic devotion, when death did come, God has granted, "that when his eyes were turned to behold for the last time the sun in heaven, they saw him shining (and with well founded faith that he would so shine for all generations to come), on our glorious Union, with the gorgeous ensign of the Republic, now known and honored throughout the earth, still full high, advanced and advancing, not a single star obscured, not a single stripe erased, and still bearing for its motto, everywhere spread all over, in characters of living light, blazing on all its ample folds, as they float over the sea and over the land, and in every wind under the heavens, that sentiment, dear to every true American, "LIBERTY AND UNION, NOW AND FOREVER, ONE AND INSEPARABLE."

J. HARDY PRINCE, Esq., paid a most glowing tribute to the memory of Mr. Webster, in a speech of great ability and eloquence, followed by J. HARRIS SMITH, Esq., who advocated the passage of the resolutions. The question upon the resolutions was then taken, and they passed unanimously.

PROCEEDINGS OF THE WEBSTER UNDER-VOTERS.

The Webster Under-Voters of this city met on Tuesday evening, October 26, to take suitable measures for a tribute to the memory of Daniel Webster. Arthur J. G. Sowdon presided. The meeting was very large, and the proceedings were characterized by that order and propriety so befitting the occasion, the place, and the young gentlemen themselves.

The following resolutions were offered by Mr. Eayres, and unanimously adopted:

Whereas, Through the dispensation of an all-wise Providence, we have been called upon to mourn the loss of that great statesman, patriot, and Christian, Daniel Webster, who has ever been to us from our earliest childhood the synonyme of all that is great and good in man — around whom we have so often delighted to gather as around a kind of parent to catch the words of wisdom and instruction which fell from his lips; whose strains of magic eloquence are to us as household words; whose lofty sentiments of patriotism have sunk so deep into our hearts that time can never erase them; — therefore,

Resolved, That in the intense grief and heartfelt sorrow which now pervade the country at the death of Daniel Webster, the Young Men of Boston would mingle their tears and join their sorrows, feeling that the loss which they have sustained is only exceeded by that which their country is compelled to mourn.

Resolved, That by the death of Daniel Webster, the brightest star in the glorious constellation of master spirits which has so long lighted up the pathway of human liberty through the world, has set forever; and the young men of Boston, living in the immediate vicinity of Bunker Hill, Lexington, and Plymouth — breathing in the spirit of patriotism with the very breath we draw; cannot but feel the most poignant grief at the irreparable loss which their country, the cause of liberty and republican institutions, have sustained.

Resolved, That we deeply sympathize with the family and friends of the illustrious deceased, in this their afflicting bereavement, and would assure them that the young men of Boston will ever entertain the liveliest emotions of gratitude for the services of him who was the defender of the Constitution and the preserver of our liberties.

Resolved, That in consideration of the great loss which has fallen upon the world at large, our country, and ourselves individually, the members of this Club will wear the usual badge of mourning on the left arm for a period of thirty days.

Resolved, That a committee of seven be appointed, to constitute with the government of the Club a Committee of Arrangements, to take such further measures as they may deem proper, to give expression to the sad feelings of this Club.

Resolved, That a copy of these resolutions be transmitted to Mrs. Webster.

Addresses were made by Messrs. SOWDON, BATES, and EAYRES.

MEETING OF THE BOSTON MERCHANTS.

The Merchants of Boston met on Monday afternoon, October 25, at the Merchants' Exchange Reading Room, to take such measures as might be deemed appropriate, in view of the death of Daniel Webster, whose life was one long devotion to the mercantile interests of Boston.

The meeting was called to order by George B. Upton, Esq., and organized by the choice of Hon. William Appleton, as President, who, on taking the chair, made a few touching and eloquent remarks upon the life, services, and death of Mr. Webster.

J. Thomas Stevenson, Esq., then proceeded to address the meeting as follows:

Gentlemen — The occasion of this meeting is eloquently told in the silent countenances of those who compose it, and calls for no louder utterance. Certainly no hurried words could either add to, or subdue the universal sorrow, whose shadows are resting upon the hearts of those who realize that the event of yesterday has removed from them a friend, a counsellor, a guide, a benefactor, a patriot.

I am requested to say to you, that the purpose

for which we have been called together, is the appointment of a committee with power to arrange for such testimonial on the part of the merchants of Boston as that event prompts.

Mr. Stevenson offered the following resolution:

Resolved, That a committee of seven be appointed by the Chair, to confer with any other committees that may be chosen by other bodies of our citizens, on the subject of a testimonial to the services of Daniel Webster.

The Chair appointed the following gentlemen as the Committee, viz.: — Messrs. Nathan Appleton, John T. Heard, Thomas B. Curtis, James K. Mills, A. W. Thaxter, Jr., Enoch Train, Levi Dowley, Thomas Gray.

The meeting was then dissolved.

PROCEEDINGS OF THE BOARD OF BROKERS.

At the regular meeting of the Board of Brokers held on Monday, October 25, the following resolutions were unanimously passed:

Whereas, by the dispensation of Divine Providence we are called to mourn the death of our illustrious fellow-citizen, Daniel Webster; —

Resolved, That we lament the loss of this great Statesman and Patriot, the intelligence of whose death has cast a cloud of sorrow over the whole community.

Resolved, As a mark of respect, the Board do now adjourn.

J. J. Soley, *Secretary.*

PROCEEDINGS OF THE MERCANTILE LIBRARY ASSOCIATION.

At a special meeting of the Board of Directors of the Mercantile Library Association of Boston, held on Monday evening, October 25, 1852, the following resolution, submitted by Mr. James A. Woolson, was unanimously adopted :

Resolved, In consequence of the intelligence we have received of the death of the Honorable Daniel Webster, Secretary of State of the United States, the President of this Association be requested to call a special meeting of the members, to take place on Wednesday evening, the 27th instant, that measures may be taken to manifest our deep regret at the loss the nation has sustained in the death of this great American Statesman.

A very large meeting of the members of this Association was held in their rooms Wednesday evening, October 27. Appropriate remarks were made by George S. Blanchard, the President, and speeches were made by L. H. Tasker, Charles G. Chase, and Henry Blanchard. The following resolutions, offered by John Stetson, were unanimously adopted :

Resolved, That the members of this Association have heard with deep grief the afflicting intelligence of the death of Mr. Webster:

an event which bereaves the country of its ablest and most comprehensive statesman; the Bar of its most distinguished leader; the great interests of peace, commerce, and union, of their noblest champion — and the whole nation of the grandest exemplar of those free institutions to whose defence his long and illustrious life was devoted.

Resolved, That in this event, we recognize the departure of a colossal mind, whose faculties, rare in their separate excellencies, and rarer still in their harmonious combination, have stamped on American history, legislation, and eloquence, the massive impress of their wisdom and power; a mind which in precision, depth, fervor, amplitude, and force, in closeness and clearness of statement, rigor of reasoning, and wide-reaching grasp of principles, and in the greatness and grandeur of soul which accompanied its most practical application to affairs, — had no rival, and has left no successor, though "it still lives" in the imperishable records of its ample and majestic wisdom.

Resolved, That while the death of such a man is so heavy a calamity to the nation as to make all public reference to private sorrow almost out of place, gratitude compels us to acknowledge that while we fully sympathize in the wide-spread sense of national loss, we have also to mourn a valuable friend and counsellor, to whom the Association is indebted for many important favors and benefits.

Resolved, That this Association will unite in any public solemnities which may take place under the auspices of the City Authorities; and the Board of Directors be requested to make all required arrangements for that purpose.

Subsequently Mr. Charles H. Allen was elected Chief Marshal of the Association on the occasion of the Funeral Solemnities.

PROCEEDINGS OF THE MECHANIC APPRENTICES LIBRARY ASSOCIATION.

THE Mechanic Apprentices Library Association held a special meeting on Wednesday evening, October 27, and the following resolutions were unanimously adopted:

Resolved, That our country has sustained an irreparable loss. That, in common with the inhabitants thereof, we mingle our heartfelt tears of sympathy and consolation with his bereaved family, and with the nation, with whose history his life has been so long interwoven.

Resolved, That the honesty of purpose and strict integrity with which he has sustained himself as a statesman and patriot, and the unwavering patriotism which he has ever manifested in the support of the Constitution, will render his name immortal; and in the hearts of the people he will "still live," after all that is mortal is no more, and when the monuments which eulogize his memory shall have crumbled to the dust.

Resolved, That the event of his death fills us all with feelings of unfeigned sadness; and, as a token of our respect to his memory, we clothe our rooms in the habiliments of mourning, and that a committee of five be appointed to carry the above into effect.

PROCEEDINGS OF MASSACHUSETTS SOCIETY OF THE CINCINNATI.

At a meeting of the Massachusetts Society of the Cincinnati, duly convened by the President of the same, the Hon. Robert G. Shaw, in Boston, October 26, 1852, for the purpose of taking measures to manifest a proper tribute of respect to the memory of the late Daniel Webster, an honorary member of said society; —

Voted, That Robert G. Shaw, the Rev. Mr. Baury, and Adams Bailey, be a committee to take into consideration what measures should be adopted; and draft such resolutions of condolence with the family of the late Daniel Webster as shall be deemed most proper.

Voted, That the members of this Society be requested to wear crape on the left arm for thirty days as a testimonial of respect for their lately deceased honorary member, Daniel Webster.

At a subsequent meeting, held November 4th, the foregoing committee submitted the following resolutions which were unanimously adopted:

When a nation is in tears, mourning under the bereaving stroke of Divine Providence, which has taken from them, by death, one of the most gifted of her sons; eminent for wisdom, and patriotism, and virtue; — who, like the Father of the Republic, knew no North, or South, East or West, but devoted himself alike, with all the powers and faculties of his noble and expansive mind, to the promotion of his country's honor, and his country's welfare; under such a bereavement, what remains, to soothe the anguish thus occasioned, while bowing in devout submission to the good pleasure of him who does not afflict willingly or grieve the children of men, but to muse on departed worth and greatness, whereby is elicited the unfeigned tribute of respect and veneration for his name, and his memory. Therefore

Resolved, That the members of the Massachusetts Society of the Cincinnati, will ever cherish a grateful remembrance of the invaluable services rendered, through a series of years, and during some of the most critical periods of the Republic's history, by their late Honorary member, Daniel Webster, in the national legislature, and more recently in the cabinet councils of the General Government of the United States, contributing, in an eminent degree, to the peace and safety, honor and prosperity of the nation, no less than to the preservation and permanence of the Union under the Federal Constitution.

Resolved, That while the members of this Society mourn, together with their fellow-citizens through the length and breadth of the land, the impressive bereavement which fills all hearts with sorrow, they most gratefully acknowledge the superintending Providence of God, in providing for the American people a succession of distinguished statesmen and ardent patriots, who have perpetuated in their purity and integrity, principles promulgated by the immortal Washington, and which the illustrious Webster most ably maintained and eloquently defended to his last beating pulse.

Resolved, That the members of the Massachusetts Society of the Cincinnati, in giving utterance to their sense of the severe calamity with which the United States has been visited in the removal of the Honorable Daniel Webster from the scenes of his earthly labors, are not unmindful of the irreparable loss sustained by those who were associated with him in the more intimate and endearing relations of private life. Ties, which nature and affection unite with such a man, must touch every nerve of sorrow, and render grief almost insupportable. Consolation, however, even under such circumstances, is mercifully extended to assuage the grief of all who mourn in the consideration of the useful life of the departed statesman, and the calmness with which he resigned his spirit in death to the God who gave it.

Resolved, That the President of the Massachusetts Society of the Cincinnati be requested to communicate to the family of the late Honorable Daniel Webster, with every expression of sympathy and condolence, a copy of the preceding preamble and resolutions, and that the Secretary cause the same to be entered upon the records.

ORDERS OF THE GOVERNOR OF MASSACHUSETTS.

OFFICIAL.

COMMONWEALTH OF MASSACHUSETTS.

General Order, No. 7.

HEAD-QUARTERS,
Boston, October 28th, 1852.

The Commander-in-Chief, having been informed that the illustrious statesman and patriot, Daniel Webster, Secretary of State of the United States, died at his residence in Marshfield, on the 24th day of October instant — orders, that minute-guns be fired at Head-Quarters, from 12 o'clock at noon to 1 o'clock in the afternoon of this day, as an expression of the public sorrow, and as a testimonial of respect for the eminent services and character of the deceased.

Major-General B. F. Edmands is charged with the execution of the above order. The Acting Quartermaster-General will furnish the necessary ammunition, on application of the officer detailed to command the detachment.

By order of his Excellency,

GEORGE S. BOUTWELL,
Governor and Commander-in-Chief.

EBENEZER W. STONE, *Adjutant-General.*

COMMONWEALTH OF MASSACHUSETTS.

HEAD-QUARTERS,
Boston, October 29th, 1852.

The Commander-in-Chief, as a further mark of respect to the memory of Daniel Webster, orders, that a Federal Salute be fired at Head-Quarters, at sunrise, Minute-guns from 12 M. to 2 P. M., and a National Salute at sunset, on the 29th instant, being the day of the funeral obsequies at Marshfield.

Major-General B. F. Edmands is charged with the execution of this order. The Acting Quartermaster-General will furnish the necessary ammunition on application of the officer detailed to command the detachment.

By command of his Excellency,

GEORGE S. BOUTWELL,
Governor and Commander-in-Chief.

PROCEEDINGS OF THE BUNKER HILL MONUMENT ASSOCIATION.

At a special meeting of the Board of Directors of the Bunker Hill Monument Association, on Wednesday, October 27, the following resolutions were passed:

Resolved, That the Directors of the Bunker Hill Monument Association do most severely sympathize in the general grief which has overwhelmed the country in the national loss which it has so unexpectedly been called upon to bear; by which sad event one of the founders and projectors of the great work of the Association has been removed from earth, the memory of whose undying eloquence uttered before a vast multitude on Bunker Hill at the laying of the corner stone of the Monument, and also at its completion, will be forever identified with that imperishable memorial to the cause of republican liberty.

Resolved, That the eminent public services of the illustrious deceased, rendered throughout his whole life, constantly, in full measure and with the most cordial readiness, at the sacrifice of his personal interest, furnish the best example of that high aim which he so eloquently set forth to his countrymen; for his whole life was to *his country, his whole country, and nothing but his country.*

Resolved, That in respect to the memory of Daniel Webster, the monument be dressed with appropriate badges of mourning for the space of thirty days, and that it be recommended to the officers and members of the Association to wear the usual badge of mourning upon the left arm for the same term.

Resolved, That the President, Secretary, and Treasurer of this Association, with Hon. Stephen Fairbanks, Hon. Nathan Hale, Hon. Albert Fearing, Joseph Tilden, Esq., Henry Forster, Esq., and Henry A. Pierce, Esq., be appointed a delegation to attend the funeral of the deceased on Friday next.

Resolved, That these resolutions be entered upon the record of the Association; that a copy of them, signed by the President and Secretary, be forwarded to the family of the deceased, and that they also be published in the journals of the day.

G. WASHINGTON WARREN, *President.*

JOSEPH H. BUCKINGHAM, *Secretary.*

PROCEEDINGS OF THE MASSACHUSETTS CHARITABLE MECHANICS' ASSOCIATION.

At a special meeting of the Massachusetts Charitable Mechanics' Association, held on the evening of October 29, the following gentlemen were appointed a Committee to report resolutions in relation to the national bereavement which has just fallen upon the American people: — Stephen Fairbanks, George Darracott, James Clark, Henry N. Hooper, John Rayner, Nathaniel Hammond, Enoch Hobart, Elijah Mears, Frederick W. Lincoln, Jr.

The Committee having retired, subsequently reported the following resolutions, which were unanimously adopted:

Resolved, That this Association shares in the general sensibility and sorrow pervading this community, at the great national loss which the country has sustained in the recent decease of its eminent Statesman and Patriot, Daniel Webster.

Resolved, That while his departure from this life casts a gloom over the hearts of our countrymen in every part of the Union, as well as upon the friends of constitutional liberty throughout the world, yet this bereavement has a deeper poignancy of grief to us who participated with him in those closer local relations growing out of a common citizenship of the same city and Commonwealth, and has also been enhanced by a still nearer bond to us in our associate capacity; as is testified in the fact that he has been for many years one of our most valued honorary members.

Resolved, That in Mr. Webster's life and career we have had the most illustrious example of the full development of genius under Republican institutions; and its influence in return, upon those institutions themselves, in their more perfect adaptation to the wants of the people in accordance with the progressive spirit of the age. His efforts in behalf of the perpetuity of the Constitution, and the sacred obligations of law — his interest in the education of the great mass of the people — his valuable services in the development of the agricultural and material resources of the country — and his devotion to the cause of manual labor and domestic industry — all these, and more of a kindred nature, to the support of which he gave his matchless eloquence, impregnated with that stanch American patriotism, worthy of the Father of the Republic, have established for him a fame unsurpassed in the world, and bequeathed to his countrymen and posterity a personal example, and the record of a consummate wisdom, which, if heeded, will secure prosperity to our beloved land, as long as it remains " a power among the nations."

Resolved, That the government be authorized to take such further measures in relation to the illustrious deceased as they may deem expedient; also, that the foregoing resolves be entered upon our records, and a copy of the same be transmitted to Mrs. Webster and her family.

After the passage of the above resolutions, it was

Voted, That the Government be requested to attend the funeral.

Jonas Chickering, *President.*

Frederick H. Stimson, *Secretary.*

PROCEEDINGS OF THE BOSTON MARINE SOCIETY.

At the Annual Meeting of the Boston Marine Society, held November 3d, the following Resolutions, offered by Thomas B. Curtis, Esq., were unanimously adopted:

Resolved, That in the death of Daniel Webster, the maritime interests of our beloved country have, in common with all other interests, lost their ablest defender. Witness his words — "The American Government, then, is prepared to say that *the practice of impressing seamen from American vessels* CANNOT HEREAFTER BE ALLOWED TO TAKE PLACE." And witness the admission made by Lord Ashburton, then representing the English Government — "I must admit that when a British subject — Irish, English, or Welsh — becomes an American, and claims no longer the protection of his own country, *his own country has no right to call him a subject, and to put him in a position to make war on his adopted country.*" This declaration and this admission entitle Daniel Webster to the gratitude of all who navigate the seas under the United States flag.

Resolved, That this Society will join in any testimonials of respect which may offer to the members an opportunity of manifesting their grief, as at the loss of a father and friend.

Resolved, That the Board of Trustees of this Society be a Committee, with full powers to make such arrangements as may best serve to carry into effect the wishes of the Society, as expressed in the foregoing resolution.

PROCEEDINGS OF THE SONS OF NEW HAMPSHIRE.

At a meeting of the Sons of New Hampshire, held November 6, 1852, the following Resolutions were unanimously adopted:

Resolved, That in the death of Daniel Webster the State of New Hampshire has lost the most eminent of her Sons, the United States their greatest Statesman, and the World one of its most distinguished Jurists.

Resolved, That, while in common with others, we have venerated him for his majestic intellect, honored him for his wise and patriotic counsels and great public services, and share in the general grief which pervades the whole country upon the occasion of this national bereavement, he has been endeared to us still more by his private virtues, the kindness of his heart, and the warmth of his affections.

Resolved, That this afflictive dispensation of Divine Providence, more especially as it has removed the officer appointed to preside at our *proposed Festival,* renders that Festival inappropriate at the present time, and that, as a token of respect to his memory, it be postponed.

Resolved, That we respectfully tender the expression of our warmest sympathies to the family and relatives of Mr. Webster, and that the Chairman be requested to transmit to them a copy of these resolutions.

A copy of Record.

R. J. Burbank, *Secretary.*

PROCEEDINGS OF THE PRESIDENT AND FELLOWS OF HARVARD COLLEGE.

At a meeting of the President and Fellows of Harvard College, held in Boston, on Saturday, October 30, 1852, the following tribute to the memory of Mr. Webster was read, and was ordered to be entered on the records, to be published in the newspapers, and communicated to the family of the deceased:

The Corporation of Harvard College, holding a stated meeting during the week of the death and the burial of Daniel Webster, cannot but feel deeply, and desire earnestly to express their sense of the loss of a man whose life was valuable in so many of the most important spheres of human occupation, who was connected with the management of Harvard College as an Overseer, for a period of thirty years, and who has secured to all American Colleges the enjoyment of the rights conferred by their charters.

Leaving to others the commemoration of his services in public life, as a statesman and a diplomatist, and in the more private, but scarcely less important position of a jurist, the Corporation deem it appropriate for them to speak, with the admiring applause it deserves, of his character as a scholar, and a man of letters, a classic writer, and a consummate orator. The discipline he imposed upon himself, from his earliest youth, in the pursuit of knowledge and skill in these departments of intellectual culture, contending with, and overcoming obstacles thrown in his way by poverty, obscurity of position, and some natural tendency to self-distrust, may well serve as an example, and his eminent success as an encouragement, to the young, to lose no moment and no opportunity for the cultivation of the faculties they may possess. Mr. Webster's wonderful powers were made available to the good of his country, and of mankind, by his industry and faithfulness in the use of them, from the earliest period at which any thing is recorded of him to the latest hour of his life; and while his talents command admiration, the warmer feelings of approbation and gratitude are excited by his devotion of them to the highest purposes. The noble example he has given of patriotism, truth, and religious fidelity to his convictions, is of immeasurable value; and his memory will be cherished by the multitudes with whom he has been associated, and by countless generations, who will know him only by the blessings they will owe.

A true copy of the record,

James Walker, *Secretary.*

PROCEEDINGS OF THE MASSACHUSETTS HISTORICAL SOCIETY.

NOVEMBER MEETING, 1852.

Voted, That Messrs. Robbins, Appleton, and Austin, be a Committee to draft a series of Resolutions appropriate to the memory of our late deceased associate, the Honorable Daniel Webster; and to report, if any, and what steps should be taken by the Society in con-consequence of his death.

Copy of record.

JOSEPH WILLARD, *Recording Secretary.*

The Committee, appointed as above, reported, at the regular meeting in December, the following preamble, resolution, and recommendation, which were unanimously adopted.

Whereas, in the course of Divine Providence, the spirit of Daniel Webster has returned to God, and the places of public honor and private friendship which knew him on earth, shall know him no more forever;—

Resolved, That the members of the Massachusetts Historical Society, while, in common with the whole American people, they mourn his loss, as an illustrious statesman, an ardent patriot, a wise counsellor, an eloquent orator, the ablest defender of the Constitution, and a great man, are desirous, also, as a Society, to express and record their tribute of respect to the high services and renowned name of an honored associate, whose matchless powers, devoted to his country, have performed such works as enrich a nation's annals, and make its history glorious.

Your Committee would further recommend, that Mr. George Ticknor be appointed to prepare a memoir of Mr. Webster, for the Society's publications.

PROCEEDINGS OF THE AMERICAN ACADEMY OF ARTS AND SCIENCES.

At a meeting of the Academy at their room in the Athenæum Building, November 1st, Professor Felton, of Harvard University, called the attention of the members present to a deceased Fellow, the Honorable Daniel Webster, by an address in the following terms:

Mr. President—I rise to suggest that the recent death of an illustrious citizen, be suitably noticed by this Academy, of which he was a Fellow. From every quarter of the country the voice of mourning and lamentation strikes upon the ear; on every side the emblems of grief meet the eye. Daniel Webster is no more, and the great heart of the nation is smitten with sorrow under so heavy a bereavement. All classes of men—all parties—all professions and occupations—join in doing honor to his memory, with a unanimity of grief unexampled since the death of the Father of his Country.

It is not my purpose or province to eulogize the man whom a nation deplores. That sad and grateful task has been performed by lips touched with the living flame of eloquence from the altar where his own eloquence was kindled. Those who stood by him longest in public life and who shared most intimately in his friendship and fireside conversation; his brethren at the Bar, where he was foremost; his associates in the Senate, where he was the first among equals; his colleagues in the Cabinet, where he was the guiding star of policy; they who have acted with him or under him, in diplomacy, — will most fittingly delineate his character, in its massive proportions and towering grandeur.

The currents of public and professional life bore him, in a measure, away from the fields of science and letters; and his winter residence, for many years at a distance from this city, deprived us of his personal coöperation in the proceedings of this Academy. Yet, in the midst of great and constant professional labors; under the weight of public duties and the cares of office, his comprehensive mind has never been alienated from the genial pursuits of letters and science. In his legal arguments and his public discourses, he has shown rich acquirements in learning, and a minute familiarity with the progress of modern discovery. In the science of government, in political philosophy, he was without a superior. The profound thoughts, matured by his luminous intellect, and given to the public through a long series of years, have become a part of the common sense of the country. He was no stranger to the walks of ancient learning. The ethical and political wisdom of Aristotle and Cicero he had deeply studied. The poem of Homer, and the histories of Herodotus, Thucydides, and Polybius, commanded his admiration, and occupied many of his leisure hours. The great Roman Masters were, in a more special manner, his daily friends and companions; and he read their works not only with an appreciation of the substance and philosophy, but with a refined discrimination of their manner and style. With the best writers in English literature, his acquaintance was profound and critical. Those who have heard him read from Shakspeare, Milton, and Gray, and converse upon them afterwards, remember, not only how deeply he entered into the spirit of these illustrious authors, but with what rare felicity of judgment and delicacy of taste he discriminated the minutest shades of beauty, in the structure of their sentences, and the choice and arrangement of their words. This fine literary taste, the result of natural gifts disciplined by study, is seen in the freshness, vigor, and beauty of his style, in his published works.

Mr. Webster was accustomed to lament that the pressure of business had limited his studies to fragmentary portions of time; and to regret that he had so seldom enjoyed, for any length of time, the society of scientific men. Yet he had not failed to keep pace with the progress of science in our age. I remember falling accidentally in his company, more than twenty years since, among the granite mountains of New Hampshire, and noticing that the book he had taken with him, on a journey of recreation, was a treatise, then just published, on the science of Geology. In a conversation I held with him just five weeks before his death, he told me that many years ago, being unable to visit remote localities, and to examine the formations *in situ*, and yet desirous to see the order of nature with his own eyes while he read, he had employed a learned geologist to make a collection of specimens, and to arrange them on shelves, according to the succession of layers in the crust of the earth. I might enumerate other sciences, the progress of which had not escaped his attention. The principles of Physical Geography, its relations to the history of man, and the distribution of the animal and vegetable kingdoms over the face of the earth, as developed by Ritter and Humboldt, were well understood by him. Among the books which occupied the last months of his life, was Humboldt's Cosmos, which he had carefully studied, mastering its substance and details with characteristic ability and comprehension. His tastes as a sportsman had led him to observe carefully the habits of the fishes of our streams and coasts, and his knowledge of them was extensive and exact. One of the plans he had laid out for the leisure he seemed about to enjoy, was to write a work, in which these observations should be recorded. The last request he made to me, in the conversation I have alluded to, was that I would submit to a member of this Academy, whose work on Fresh-water Fishes he had recently examined, certain questions relating to some of the phenomena of Ichthyology, which he had noticed, but did not fully understand.

I have thought, Mr. President, that the character and works of this distinguished person were such that his associates in this Academy would deem it fitting to notice the Dispensation of Providence which has taken him away. I am persuaded it will be the dictate of every heart,—if I may borrow the words of one of his favorite authors,—"Sic memoriam venerari, ut omnia facta dictaque ejus secum revolvant, formamque ac figuram animi magis quam corporis complectantur. Forma mentis æterna. Quidquid ex eo amavimus, quidquid mirati sumus, manet, mansurumque est, in animis hominum, in æternitate temporum, fama rerum."

I ask leave to offer the following resolutions:

Resolved, That the Fellows of the American Academy of Arts and Sciences deeply lament the decease of their late associate, the Honorable Daniel Webster, Secretary of State of the United States. By his death the Country is bereaved of her ablest practical statesman, and profoundest political philosopher; Letters and Eloquence have lost a most distinguished ornament; Science is deprived of a great and versatile mind, which understood its progress, appreciated its value, recognized its dignity, and mastered its results, in the midst of professional labors and public cares, to which his energies were devoted almost to the last moment of his life.

Resolved, That the Fellows of this Academy tender to the family of their late eminent associate their most respectful sympathy, in this private and public calamity.

The resolutions were seconded by the Hon. Francis C. Gray, who made some remarks, and by Professor Parsons, of the Cambridge Law School, who spoke in their support; and they were unanimously adopted.

FUNERAL.

THE FUNERAL.

Friday, October 29, was the day of Mr. Webster's funeral. Boston never before presented — probably never will again present — so general an aspect of mourning, and never were there witnessed such spontaneous, universal, and deep tokens of feeling. Most of the shops were closed, as well as the public institutions, offices, and markets ; and a large proportion of the city was dressed in the habiliments of sorrow. The mourning draperies upon many of the buildings, public and private, were rich, elaborate, and tasteful. Festoons of black and white were almost continuous through Washington, Hanover, and other principal streets ; and multiplied mottoes, expressing grief and admiration, were placed upon walls and over door-ways. Flags, prepared with inscriptions and dressed in mourning, were extended across the streets. In general, the mottoes and inscriptions were extremely well chosen and appropriate, and were a proof, not only of the estimation in which Mr. Webster was held in Boston, but of the high standard of taste and cultivation among its citizens.

In the multiplicity of these personal and spontaneous expressions of feeling, it is impossible to describe, or specify any; but from amongst the mottoes, of which more than a hundred were exhibited, the following are selected:

His words of wisdom, with resistless power,
Have graced our brightest, cheered our darkest hour.

Thou hast instructed many, and thou hast strengthened the weak hands.

We've scanned the actions of his daily life and nothing meets our eyes but deeds of honor.

Some when they die, die all. Their mouldering clay is but an emblem of their memories. But he has lived. He leaves a work behind which will pluck the shining age from vulgar time, and give it whole to late posterity.

Thou art mighty yet. Thy spirit walks abroad.

The great heart of the nation throbs heavily at the portals of his grave.

Live like patriots! Live like Americans! United all, united now, and united forever.

Wherever among men a heart shall be found that beats to the transports of patriotism and liberty, its aspirations shall be to claim kindred with his spirit.

Then this Daniel was preferred above the Presidents and Princes, because an excellent spirit was in him.

Know thou, O stranger, to the fame
Of this much loved, much honored name,
(For none that knew him need be told,)
A warmer heart Death ne'er made cold.

The glory of thy life, like the day of thy death, shall not fail from the remembrance of man.

Between twelve and one — the hour of the funeral

at Marshfield — minute guns were fired, and the bells of the churches were tolled; from sunrise to sunset guns were fired every fifteen minutes, and almost continuously. Similar signs of mourning were heard from the hills of the neighboring towns, and along the line of the coast. The streets were crowded with citizens and visitors from the country, reading the inscriptions, and walking through the public buildings, all wearing, upon their saddened countenances, tokens of sincere sorrow. Though a day of leisure and entire cessation from labor, there was no thought of any thing but our great loss. There were no smiling faces to be seen, and no cheerful voices to be heard.

The funeral solemnities were at Mr. Webster's own residence in Marshfield. In conformity with the wish expressed in his will, every thing was arranged with the utmost simplicity, in the order usual in a New England funeral, but private it could not be. In addition to the general sense of loss in the removal of a great leader and a statesman, in whose wisdom and firmness so strong a confidence was reposed, there was in many hearts a feeling of personal bereavement in the death of a revered and beloved friend; and thus thousands were led to the spot by a wish to honor his memory and look once more upon his face. From all quarters, by every path, and by every conveyance, great multitudes came together; and the whole number of persons assembled at the hour of noon was probably not less than ten or twelve thousand.

A thoughtful consideration for the feelings of all who were present was shown in the arrangements of the funeral. In order that the wish which all felt, to look for the last time upon the face of the illustrious dead, might be gratified without hurry or confusion, the body was brought from the library at an early hour in the morning and placed upon the lawn, in front of the house, beneath the open heavens and under a tree which, in its summer foliage, was a conspicuous ornament of the spot. The majestic form reposed in the familiar garb of life, with more than the dignity of life in its most imposing moments. Suffering had changed, without impairing those noble features. The grandeur of the brow was untouched, and the attitude full of strength and peace. For more than three hours a constant stream of men and women, of all ages, passed on both sides, pausing for a moment to look upon that loved and honored form. Parents held their children by the hand, bade them contemplate the face of their benefactor, and charged them never to lose the memory of that spectacle and that hour. Many dissolved into tears as they turned aside; and one—a man of plain garb and appearance—was heard to make, in a subdued voice, the striking remark, "Daniel Webster, the world will seem lonesome without you."

The thoughtful and kindly feeling which dictated all the arrangements, permitted any who wished, to enter the house by the principal entrance, walk through a small sitting-room, where hang several family portraits, and going through the library, a beautiful and favorite room, ornamented with the likenesses of Mr. Webster and Lord Ashburton, pass out upon the lawn. Thousands availed themselves of this privilege,—silently, decorously, sadly. There was no sound from that vast multitude, but the inevitable grating of their feet upon the paths. This was like the chafing of the surf upon a pebbly beach,—a strange, impressive murmur.

At twelve, the passing through the house was stopped. Soon afterwards, the Rev. EBENEZER ALDEN, pastor of the Congregational Church in South Marshfield, where Mr. Webster had been accustomed to attend public worship, commenced the religious service by reading a selection from the Bible. After which, the following address was made by him:

On an occasion like the present, a multitude of words were worse than idle. Standing before that majestic form, it becomes ordinary men to keep silence. "He being dead, yet speaketh." In the words he applied to Washington, in the last great public discourse he ever delivered, the whole atmosphere is redolent of his name; hills and forests, rocks and rivers, echo and reëcho his praises. All the good, whether learned or unlearned, high or low, rich or poor, feel this day that there is one treasure common to them all, and that is the fame and character of Webster. They recount his deeds, ponder over his principles and teachings, and resolve to be more and more guided by them in future. Americans by birth are proud of his character, and exiles from foreign shores are eager to participate in admiration of him; and it is true that he is, this day, here, everywhere, more an object of love and regard than on any day since his birth.

And while the world, too prone to worship mere intellect, laments that the orator and statesman is no more, we enter upon more sacred ground, and dwell upon the example and counsels of a *Christian*, as a husband, father, and friend. I trust it will be no rude wounding of the spirit, no intrusion upon the privacy of domestic life, to allude to a few circumstances in the last scenes of the mortal existence of the great man who is gone, fitted to administer Christian consolation, and to guide to a better acquaintance with that religion which is adapted both to temper our grief and establish our hope.

Those who were present upon the morning of that Sabbath upon which this head of a family conducted the worship of his household, will never forget, as he read from our Lord's Sermon on the Mount, the emphasis which he alone was capable of giving to that passage which speaks of the divine nature of forgiveness. They saw beaming from that eye, now closed in death, the Spirit of Him who first uttered that godlike sentiment.

And he who, by the direction of the dying man, upon a subsequent morning of the day of rest, read in their connection these words: "Lord, I believe; help thou my unbelief;" and then the closing chapter of our Saviour's last words to his disciples, being particularly requested to dwell upon this clause of the verse—"Holy Father, keep through thine own name those whom thou hast given me, that they may be one as we are"—beheld a sublime illustration of the indwelling and abiding power of Christian faith.

And if these tender remembrances only cause our

tears to flow more freely, it may not be improper for us to present the example of the father, when his great heart was rent by the loss of a daughter whom he most dearly loved. Those present on that occasion well remember when the struggle of mortal agony was over, retiring from the presence of the dead, bowing together before the presence of God, and joining with the afflicted father as he poured forth his soul, pleading for grace and strength from on high.

As upon the morning of his death we conversed upon the evident fact that, for the last few weeks, his mind had been engaged in preparation for an exchange of worlds, one who knew him, well remarked, "His whole life has been that preparation." The people of this rural neighborhood, among whom he spent the last twenty years of his life, among whom he died, and with whom he is to rest, have been accustomed to regard him with mingled veneration and love. Those who knew him best, can the most truly appreciate the lessons both from his lips and example, teaching the sustaining power of the Gospel.

His last words, "I STILL LIVE," we may interpret in a higher sense than that in which they are usually regarded. He has taught us how to attain the life of faith and the life to come.

Vividly impressed upon the memory of the speaker is the instruction once received as to the fitting way of presenting divine truth from the sacred desk. Would that its force might be felt by those who are called to minister in divine things. Said Mr. Webster, "When I attend upon the preaching of the Gospel, I wish to have it made *a personal matter*, A PER-

SONAL MATTER, A PERSONAL MATTER." It is to present him as enforcing these divine lessons of wisdom and consolation, that we have recalled to your minds these precious recollections.

And we need utter no apology. Indeed, we should be inexcusable in letting the present opportunity pass without unveiling the inner sanctuary of the life of the foremost man of all this world; for his most intimate friends are well aware that he had it in mind to prepare a work upon the internal evidences of Christianity, as a testimony of his heartfelt conviction of the "divine reality" of the Gospel of Jesus Christ. But, finding himself rapidly approaching those august scenes of immortality into which he had so often looked, he dictated the most important part of his epitaph. And so long as "the rock shall guard his rest, and the ocean sound his dirge," the world shall read upon his monument, not only

> One of the few, the immortal names,
> Which were not born to die;

but also that Daniel Webster lived and died in the Christian faith. The delineation which he gave of one of his early and noble compeers, could never have been written except from an experimental acquaintance with that which he holds up as the chief excellence of his friend. This description we shall apply to himself, trusting that it will be as well understood as admired.

Political eminence and professional fame fade away and die with all things earthly. Nothing of character is really permanent but virtue and personal worth.

These remain. Whatever of excellence is wrought into the soul itself belongs to both worlds. Real goodness does not attach itself merely to this life; it points to another world. Political or professional reputation cannot last forever; but a conscience void of offence before God and man is an inheritance for eternity. Religion, therefore, is a necessary and indispensable element in any great human character. There is no living without it. Religion is the tie that connects man with his Creator, and holds him to His throne. If that tie be all sundered, all broken, he floats away, a worthless atom in the universe; its proper attractions all gone, its destiny thwarted, and its whole future nothing but darkness, desolation, and death. A man with no sense of religious duty is he whom the Scriptures describe in such terse but terrific language, as living without God in the world. Such a man is out of his proper being, out of the circle of all his duties, out of the circle of all his happiness, and away, far, far away from the purposes of his creation.

A mind like Mr. Webster's, active, thoughtful, penetrating, sedate, could not but meditate deeply on the condition of man below, and feel its responsibilities. He could not look on this mighty system,

> This universal frame, thus wondrous fair,

without feeling that it was created and upheld by an Intelligence, to which all other intelligence must be responsible. I am bound to say that in the course of my life I never met with an individual, in any profession or condition, who always spoke and always thought with such awful reverence of the power and presence of God. No irreverence, no lightness, even no too familiar allusion to God and his attributes ever escaped his lips. The very notion of a Supreme Being was, with him, made up of awe and solemnity. It filled the whole of his great mind with the strongest emotions. A man like him, with all his proper sentiments and sensibilities alive in him, must, in this state of existence, have something to believe, and something to hope for; or else, as life is advancing to its close, all is heart-sinking and oppression. Depend upon it, whatever may be the mind of an old man, old age is only really happy when, on feeling the enjoyments of this world pass away, it begins to lay a stronger hold on the realities of another.

Mr. Webster's religious sentiments and feelings were the crowning glories of his character.

The address was followed by a prayer. The rooms, hall, and stairway, were filled by Mr. Webster's relatives and friends, while a vast mass of listeners stood on the piazza, and on the lawn; the position of the clergyman, near the hall door, enabling many to hear.

During the exercises, unperceived by the group round the clergyman, arrangements were made for conveying the body to the tomb. The metallic case, in which it was deposited, was covered, and placed on a simple, low platform, drawn by one pair of black horses, whose harness was slightly dressed with crape. The coffin was covered with full black cloth, confined by several plated ornaments; a wreath of oak leaves was at the head; another of fresh flowers at the foot.

After a few moments' pause, at the conclusion of the prayer, two or three gentlemen quietly and gradually opened a path through the dense mass of persons around the house. In solemn silence, six of Mr. Webster's neighbors, Asa Hewett, Seth Weston, Eleazer Harlow, J. P. Cushman, Tilden Ames, Daniel Phillips, took their places on either side of his bier. His son, grandson, relatives, domestics, and the persons having the charge and management of his estates, stood next. Among the domestics were several colored persons, who had been long in Mr. Webster's service, and were deeply attached to him. One of them had been recently emancipated by him. The Governor of the Commonwealth, the Council and State Officers, the Mayor of Boston and City Government, distinguished citizens of Massachusetts, and many from the other New England States, and delegations from other States and cities, with hundreds of personal, devoted friends of Mr. Webster, quietly passed into the long sad procession ; truly a sad procession ; for the multitudes that lined the path for nearly the whole distance to the tomb, were moved by the same grief that rested on the hearts of the mourners.

The morning had been uncommonly beautiful. The air was soft and warm, and the light so rich and golden, that the slight shade still found under some few trees, had been grateful. Just as the procession began to move, a chill breeze came up from the ocean, and threw a veil of mist over the sky.

When the funeral train, all on foot, unheralded by official pomp, military display, or even the strains of mourning music, had reached the modest tomb, the honored form was rested at the entrance. It was once more uncovered that relatives and friends might again and for the last time, look upon that majestic countenance; a fervent prayer was again offered; and then, slowly and sadly, friend and stranger passed away, and left the illustrious sleeper with those whom he had so tenderly loved in life, and with whom death had now reunited him.

The tomb, with its group of unpretending monuments, is on a gentle eminence, about a mile from the mansion-house, and adjoining the ancient village burying-ground, where rests the dust of some of the early Pilgrim Fathers. Mr. Webster had himself superintended the preparation of the tomb, and the erection of the monuments to the wife and children he had lost, directing that the one erected to himself should be of the same style and proportions. Over the door of the tomb is cut merely, "Daniel Webster." On the three monuments within the inclosure, are the following inscriptions:

GRACE FLETCHER,
Wife of Daniel Webster,
Born January 16, 1781,
Died January 21, 1828.
Blessed are the pure in heart, for they shall see God.

JULIA WEBSTER,
wife of
Samuel Appleton Appleton;
Born January 16, 1818,
Died April 28, 1848,
Let me go, for the day breaketh.

MARY CONSTANCE APPLETON,
Born Feb. 7, 1848.
Died March 15, 1849.

MAJOR EDWARD WEBSTER,
Born July 20, 1820.
Died at San Angel, in Mexico,
In the military service
of his country,
Jan. 23, 1848.
A dearly beloved son and brother.

As the multitude turned from the hallowed spot, many gathered flowers, leaves, or even blades of grass, to be treasured as memorials of a day, unequalled in solemn pathos, within their experience. The effect upon the minds of all present, can never be described.

All things were in harmony, — the beauty of the day, the falling leaves, the countenances of the assembled multitude, the appropriate arrangements, the aspect of the autumnal landscape, — all aided in producing an elevated and tender mood of feeling. It was one of those rare occasions in which a brief space of time is sufficient to leave impressions, which all the experiences of future life will not be able to efface.

PROCESSION AND SERVICES

ON THE

THIRTIETH OF NOVEMBER.

PROCESSION AND SERVICES ON THE THIRTIETH OF NOVEMBER.

Tuesday, November 30th, was the day devoted by the City Authorities of Boston, to a public expression of respect for the memory of Mr. Webster. The day was highly favorable, the weather being mild, and the air clear. The common business of the city, was suspended, and the streets were filled with a concourse of spectators, whose manner and appearance showed their sense of the great loss they had sustained.

The New Hampshire Legislature had voted to attend the obsequies; and, at an early hour in the morning, the Executive Committee of the Sons of New Hampshire, and other natives of the State, assembled at the Depot of the Lowell Railroad, in order to receive them.

The Concord train came in at a quarter after nine o'clock, with about two hundred and fifty members of the Council, Senate, and House of Representatives. Hon. John S. Wells, President of the New Hampshire Senate, Governor Martin being detained by indisposition, was introduced to Hon. Marshall P. Wilder, President of the Executive Committee of the Sons of New Hampshire, in Boston, by Mr. Wiggin, of Dover, of the Committee of Arrangements. After the introduction, Colonel WILDER addressed Mr. Wells, as the representative of his State, as follows:

Mr. President of the Senate, and Gentlemen — In behalf of the Sons of New Hampshire, resident in Boston and vicinity, I bid you welcome to this city, and to the State of our adoption.

The afflictive dispensation of Providence which has assembled us together this morning, and the objects of our meeting are so well known by all, as to need only a brief explanation from me.

A mighty one has fallen! Our elder brother, New Hampshire's favorite son, is no more! All that was mortal of Daniel Webster, the great American Expounder of Constitutional authority and National rights, has been consigned to the bosom of his mother earth.

The loss to us, to the country, and the world, is irreparable. The whole nation mourns. Our city is hung in the drapery of woe, "and the mourners go about the streets."

New Hampshire claims the honor of Mr. Webster's birth; and among the millions who are afflicted in the general bereavement, none, I am sure, are more sincere mourners, than her sons. As brethren of the same family, we receive you with true fraternal affection; and we unite our sympathy and mingle our tears with yours.

But in this hour of our trial and sorrow, let us not forget that our loss is his unspeakable gain. Although we now mourn, let us thank God that he was spared to us so long, that he was enabled to accomplish so much for us, and for the cause of universal freedom and humanity, and that his sun was permitted to go down unclouded, and shining in the greatness of its strength.

Gentlemen, it is not my province to pronounce his eulogy; that duty will be performed by abler men, and more gifted lips.

Daniel Webster is dead! We shall see that majestic form no more! But his fame is immortal! It is registered on the hearts of his grateful countrymen. Yes, and it shall be transmitted unsullied and untarnished through all coming ages; and when the monumental marble shall have crumbled into dust, it shall "*still live!*" It shall LIVE FOREVER!

To which, Hon. JOHN S. WELLS replied, in behalf of the New Hampshire Delegation:

Mr. President and Gentlemen, "Sons of New Hampshire" — The representatives of the people of New Hampshire have postponed, for this day, their official duties, that they may join the citizens of Massachusetts in doing honor to the memory of him, whose birthplace, like yours, was surrounded by the wild scenery of our mountains, but whose fame is limited only by the bleak regions of ignorance and barbarism. We thank you, gentlemen, for your kind civilities to us on this occasion, and trust that the impressions of this day may induce in us a warmer love for our native State, and a more ardent desire for the preservation of our common country

The bodies then formed in procession, under direction of Mr. Cheney, Chief Marshal of the "Sons," and proceeded to the State House, where the guests from New Hampshire were introduced to Governor Boutwell and the Executive Council, by Mr. Wilder, and the GOVERNOR made the following address:

Mr. President, and Gentlemen of the Executive and Legislative Departments of New Hampshire — Occasions of mourning come to communities and nations as they do to individuals and families of the human race. This is an unusual assemblage. Massachusetts and New Hampshire have together passed through scenes of trial and suffering, and together have enjoyed the nation's triumphs and participated in the nation's prosperity. But now, in the general bereavement, they are peculiarly afflicted. New Hampshire has had no such other son; Massachusetts has had no such other citizen as Daniel Webster. Amid the solemnities of death, the differences of life shall be forgotten, and from the common grief shall spring sentiments of patriotism and religion, whose influence shall be felt in coming centuries of our country's existence. Gentlemen, we accept your presence as an elevated token of respect for the illustrious dead, and as an assurance that, with the other States of this confederacy, our principles, our hopes, our destiny, are one.

President WELLS responded as follows:

Sir — In the absence of his Excellency, Governor Martin, who is prevented by illness from joining us on this occasion, allow me to say, that the several branches of the Legislature of New Hampshire have met your Excellency and the citizens of Massachusetts here to-day, to join in the ceremonies to be observed by you, in honor of the memory of the late Daniel Webster.

The sable drapery of the legislative halls, from which we this morning departed, exhibits the outward signs of that sadness which pervades not only the hearts of the members of the New Hampshire Legislature, but of the sons of New Hampshire everywhere, on account of this national bereavement. They, with you, lament the fall of the illustrious Webster. His fame belongs to the nation. His birthplace was amid our mountains; he was trained in the rigid discipline of New Hampshire schools; and went forth from his native State majestic in person and mind, towering above all competition, even as our famed Mount Washington towers above all surrounding objects, and fell not till his splendid mind was recognized as one of the brightest, loftiest intellects of earth. And we have come here to-day to give force, if possible, to the hand which shall inscribe on the brazen tablets the record of his mental greatness.

Though a large majority of this body disagreed with him in the leading political doctrines of his life, yet, as an orator, a scholar, and a jurist, they have ever referred to him with pride and satisfaction; and when the black cloud of disunion was seen in the distance, and angry, convulsive feelings were aroused throughout our land, they gladly listened to the voice of Webster as it rang clear and powerful above the excited elements, urging his countrymen to the patriotic duty of standing by the Union and the Constitution. Then it was, sir, that the mass of New Hampshire hearts were turned warmly towards him. That act of patriotic devotion to his country swept into forgetfulness years of political hostility. And when it was told us that his great light was sinking beneath the horizon of life, the freemen of New Hampshire mingled their thankfulness of heart with their patriotic countrymen, that he could depart with the assurance that he left but few "seeking to look beyond the Union, to see what might lie hidden in the dark recess behind."

They sincerely rejoiced that when, for the "last time, he turned his eyes to behold the sun in heaven, he did not see it shining on the broken and dishonored fragments of a once glorious Union." But that his "last and lingering glance did behold the gorgeous ensign of the Republic, now known and honored throughout the earth, not a stripe erased or polluted, not a single star obscured, bearing not for its motto the miserable interrogatory, *What is all this worth?* but that other sentiment, dear to every true American heart, Liberty *and* Union, now and forever, one and inseparable."

The two bodies then separated to join in the procession.

The different civic bodies which turned out, assembled in due season at the several points assigned to them, and at half-past eleven o'clock the procession was brought into line, and soon after put in motion, from the City Hall, marching up Tremont street in the following order:

Military Escort, under command of
Brigadier-General Samuel Andrews.
Suffolk Brass Band.

Battalion of Cavalry, under command of Major J. T. Pierce.

National Lancers .... Capt. Jepson.
Light Dragoons .... Capt. Wright.

Salem Brass Band.

Artillery Regiment, (with mounted field-pieces), under command of Col. Cowdin.

Washington Artillery .... Capt. Bullock.
Boston Artillery........................ Capt. Evans.
Cowdin Phalanx .... Capt. Wardwell.
Roxbury Artillery .... Capt. Webber.
Columbian Artillery .... Lieut. Doherty.
Gloucester Artillery .... Capt. Cook.
Lynn Artillery .... Capt. Herbert.

Brigade Band.

Regiment of Light Infantry, under command of Col. Holbrook.

Pulaski Guards .... Capt. Wright.
City Guards .... Capt. French.
New England Guards .... Capt. Henshaw.
Boston Light Guard .... Lieut. Coverly.
Independent Fusileers .... Capt. Mitchell.
National Guard .... Lieut. Walker.
Washington Light Guard .... Capt. Flagg.
Boston Light Infantry .... Capt. Ashley.

Col. Green and Staff.

Cambridge City Guards .... Capt. Meecham.
Richardson Guards .... Lieut. Dearborn.
Stoneham Light Guard .... Capt. Dyke.
Winchester Light Guards .... Capt. Prince.
Mechanic Riflemen .... Capt. Adams.
Veteran Association .... Capt. Calfe.

Then came Gen. John S. Tyler, Chief Marshal of the day, and his Aids, followed by some forty carriages, containing the Municipal Authorities and many distinguished citizens, the Mayor and City Council of Roxbury, the Postmaster, Collector of the Port and Naval

Officer of Boston, the Judges of the United States and State Courts, Foreign Consuls, and officers of the United States Navy.

Next came the Independent Cadets, under command of Colonel T. C. Amory, accompanied by the Winchester Brass Band, as a guard of honor to his Excellency the Governor and the Executive Council; followed by the Boston School Committee, the Sergeant-at-Arms, Senators and Representatives of Massachusetts, and the Webster Executive Committee.

The third division was headed by the Newton Brass Band, and contained the members of the New Hampshire Legislature, the City Government of Charlestown, and a delegation from Springfield.

The fourth division was headed by the Lowell Brass Band, and contained the "Sons of New Hampshire," "Massachusetts Society of Cincinnati," (in carriages,) the "Cape Cod Association," with the Braintree Brass Band, the "Massachusetts Charitable Mechanic Association," and the "Mercantile Library Association," with the American Brass Band. The banner of the Sons of New Hampshire was of white satin, fringed with black, and contained on the front a striking likeness of Daniel Webster, over which was the motto, "I Still Live," and below it were the words, "I speak to-day for the preservation of the Union." On one side of the portrait, a figure of the Goddess of Liberty held a green wreath over the head of Webster; on the other was the national eagle, scroll, and motto. Below was the coat-of-arms of the State of New Hampshire, and the national shield, and at the botton was printed, "Sons of New Hampshire." On the reverse was, "One Country, one Constitution, one Destiny." "The ends I shall aim at, shall be my Country's, my God's, and Truth's."

The fifth division contained the "Scots' Charitable Society," and was headed by the Roxbury Brass Band, and a Highland piper. On one banner of this Society was inscribed,

> Wide o'er the naked world declare
> The worth we've lost.

"Boston Irish Protestant Mutual Relief Society," with a banner bearing the words—"The Immortal Webster;" on the reverse, "The Immortal Wellington." The "French Mutual Relief Society," with a banner inscribed "Daniel Webster, fut un grand homme: Français, honorons sa memoire," on the reverse, "Daniel Webster—Thy name will ever be dear to our memory." The "United Shamrock Society" was accompanied by the East Boston Brass Band, and the "Boston Roman Catholic Mutual Relief Society" followed.

The sixth division was headed by the Boston Brass Band, and contained citizens of Charlestown, three out-of-town Fire Companies, the "Bunker Hill Boys," and the "Sons of Maine," in strong force.

The seventh division was headed by the Dedham Brass Band, and contained the "Mechanic Apprentices' Library Association," the "Boston Boys' Webster Club," with a banner inscribed, "A nation's gratitude—the choicest gift of a people," and on the reverse, "I still live"—"Webster for the Union." The "Jamaica Plain Boys" bore a banner inscribed "Vivat Vivetque."

The eighth division was headed by the Easton Brass Band, and contained various Associations. The Cavalcade composed the ninth division, embracing horsemen from various adjacent towns and cities.

The solemn train passed through Tremont, Boylston, Pleasant, Washington, and Oak streets, Harrison Avenue to Beach, Lincoln, Summer, Winter, Park, Beacon, Joy, Mount Vernon, Hancock, Cambridge, Court, and Sudbury streets, across Haymarket Square to Blackstone, Hanover, Court, and State to Commercial and South Market streets to Faneuil Hall, where it arrived about two o'clock.

The procession consumed rather more than an hour in passing each point on the route. The number of persons in the column — exclusive of the military, cavalcade, and those in carriages, — by actual count amounted to more than two thousand. The number in the cavalcade was about four hundred, and in carriages between two and three hundred. Including the military, therefore, the whole procession probably numbered not far from four thousand. It proceeded generally in good order and without confusion, and its quiet passage was observed by the spectators in solemn silence.

The buildings on the route of the procession were very generally decorated with the symbols of mourning. Black and white drapery was used with good effect, and, in many places, busts and portraits of Mr. Webster were displayed.

The appearance of Faneuil Hall was highly solemn and impressive. Heavy folds of woollen cloth covered the ceiling, fastened in the centre by a silver star. The pillars were wholly cased in the same material, which also passed along the front of the encircling gallery. To this covering of the balustrade of the gallery was attached another mass of black cloth, bearing, in large gilded letters, the following inscriptions, being sentences from Mr. Webster's Works. In front of the north gallery were the words, "OUR COUNTRY, OUR WHOLE COUNTRY, AND NOTHING BUT OUR COUNTRY." In front of the eastern gallery, the words—"LIBERTY AND UNION, NOW AND FOREVER, ONE AND INSEPARABLE," were inscribed; and in front of the south gallery the words —"WE TURN TO HIS TRANSCENDENT NAME FOR COURAGE AND CONSOLATION." The clock was wholly covered, and the folds of the drapery, hanging from the back of the eagle, were so arranged as to form a niche, where a bust of Mr. Webster, by Mr. Ball, was placed.

No pictures were visible but the large one, by Mr. Healey, representing Mr. Webster in the Senate, replying to Mr. Hayne, which hangs at the end of the hall, and the portraits of Washington and Faneuil. The frames were entirely concealed by black cloth. Mr. Healey's picture was illuminated by lights from below, so arranged as to throw their full force upon the figure of Mr. Webster, producing a striking and beautiful effect. Under this picture, the words "WE CLAIM HIM FOR AMERICA" were inscribed in gilt letters. Upon the rostrum, which was raised and extended for the occasion, was placed a marble bust of Mr. Webster by Mr. King. It stood upon a pedestal about five feet high, and excited general admiration. On each side of the platform were displayed small American flags, craped.

Daylight was entirely excluded; and a row of gas-burners along the front of the galleries, two on the platform, and two large candelabra of candles also on the platform, supplied its place with a calm, subdued, yet unnatural light, which deepened the solemn effect of the whole scene. The spirit of silence and reverence pervaded the Hall, so that, at noon, when ladies were admitted, the side galleries devoted to them were filled, with little sound. Soon after, the musicians and singers took their places in the east gallery, adding to the picturesqueness and peculiarity of the scene, by moving about with lighted candles, which brought out some objects and made shadows deeper.

At a little before two, the music of the escort was heard approaching, and the Marshals, having charge of the Hall, ranged themselves at the door. The band of the Germanians breathed forth Handel's solemn march in Saul; and slowly, as if entering a mausoleum, the first division of the procession came in. Gradually, noiselessly, the numbers increased,—so gradually, that groups stood separately a moment or two gazing round at the unaccustomed sight,—the funeral hangings, the dim galleries, closely filled with undistinguishable figures, the circle of lights, and that majestic form which, from the canvas even, seemed ready to speak in words of wisdom and power. Slowly and reverently the multitude increased. The rapid rush, the noisy step, the loud exclamation, so familiar on that floor, were wholly absent. The entire space was soon filled, and a motionless sea of heads was turned to the platform, while a prayer was offered by the Rev. Dr. Lothrop. The Handel and Haydn Society then chanted one of Handel's anthems. At its conclusion, the eulogy was pronounced by Mr. Hillard; and, after a benediction, the audience dispersed.

MR. HILLARD'S EULOGY.

CITY OF BOSTON.

In Common Council, Dec. 2, 1852.

Ordered, That the thanks of the City Council be presented to the Hon. George S. Hillard, for the eloquent, impressive, and instructive Eulogy on the Life and Services of the Honorable Daniel Webster, late Secretary of State of the United States, which was delivered in Faneuil Hall before the Government and citizens of Boston, on the 30th ultimo; and that he be requested to furnish a copy for publication.

Sent up for concurrence.

Henry J. Gardner, *President.*

In Board of Mayor and Aldermen, Dec. 4, 1852.

Passed in concurrence.

Benjamin Seaver, *Mayor.*

A true copy. Attest.

Samuel F. McCleary, Jr., *City Clerk.*

EULOGY.

It is now twenty-six years since the heart of the nation was so deeply moved by the death of two great founders of the Republic, on the fiftieth anniversary of the day when its independence was declared. Then, for the first time, these consecrated walls wore the weeds of mourning. Then the multitude that filled this hall were addressed by a man, whose thoughts rose without effort to the height of his great theme. He seemed inspired by the occasion, and he looked and spoke like one on whom the mantle of some ascended prophet had at that moment fallen. He lifted up and bore aloft his audience on the wings of his mighty eloquence. His words fell upon his hearers with irresistible, subduing power, and their hearts poured themselves forth in one deep and strong tide of patriotic and reverential feeling.

And now he, that was then so full of life and power, has gone to join the patriots whom he commemorated. Webster is no more than Adams and Jefferson. The people, that then came to listen to him, are now here to mourn for him. His voice of wisdom and eloquence is silent. The arm on which a nation leaned is stark and cold. That heroic form is given back to the dust. We, that delighted to honor him in life, are now here to honor him in death. One circle of duties is ended and another is begun. We can no longer give him our confidence, our support, our suffrages; but memory and gratitude are still left to us. As he has not lived for himself alone, so he has not died for himself alone. The services of his life are crowned and sealed with the benediction of his death. So long as a man remains upon earth, his life is a fragment. It is exposed to chance and change, to the shocks of fate and the assaults of trial. But the end crowns the work. A career that is closed becomes a firm possession and a completed power. The arch is imperfect till the hand of death has fixed the keystone.

The custom of honoring great public benefactors by these solemn observances is natural, just, and wise. But the tributes and testimonials which we offer to departed worth, are for the living, and not for the dead. Eulogies, monuments, and statues can add nothing to the peace and joy of that serene sphere, into which the great and good, who have finished their earthly career, have passed. But these expressions and memorials do good to those from whom they flow. They lift us above the region of low cares and selfish struggles. They link the present to the past, and the world of sense to the world of thought. They break the common course of life with feelings brought from a higher region. Who can measure the effect of a scene like this, — these mourning walls, these saddened faces, those solemn strains of music? The seed of a deep emotion here planted, may ripen into the fruit of noble action.

A great man is a gift, in some measure, a revelation of God. A great man, living for high ends, is the divinest thing that can be seen on earth. The value and interest of history are derived chiefly from the lives and services of the eminent men whom it commemorates. Indeed, without these, there would be no such thing as history, and the progress of a nation would be as little worth recording, as the march of a trading caravan across a desert. The death of Mr. Webster is too recent, and he was taken away too suddenly from a sphere of wide and great influence, for the calm verdict of history to be passed upon him, and an accurate gauge to be taken of his works and his claims. But all men, whatever may have been the countenance they turned towards him in life, now feel that he was a man of the highest order of greatness, and that whatever of power, faculty, and knowledge there was in him, was given freely, heartily, and faithfully, during a long course of years, to the service of his country. He, who in the judgment of all, was a great man and a great patriot, not only deserves these honors at our hands, but it would be disgraceful in us to withhold them. We, among whom he lived, who felt the power of his magnificent presence, — his brow, his eye, his voice, his bearing, — can never put him anywhere but in the front rank of the great men of all time. In running along the line of statesmen and orators, we light upon the name of no one to whom we are willing to admit his inferiority.

The theory that a great man is merely the product of his age, is rejected by the common sense and common observation of mankind. The power that guides large masses of men, and shapes the channels in which the energies of a great people flow, is something more than a mere aggregate of derivative forces. It is a compound product, in which the genius of the man is one element, and the sphere opened to him by the character of his age and the institutions of his country, is another. In the case of Mr. Webster, we have a full coöperation of these two elements. Not only did he find opportunities for his great powers, but the events of his life, and the discipline through which he passed, were well fitted to train him up to that commanding intellectual stature, and perfect intellectual symmetry, which have made him so admirable, so eminent, and so useful a person.

He was fortunate in the accident, or rather the providence, of his birth. His father was a man of uncommon strength of mind and worth of character, who had served his country faithfully in trying times, and earned, in a high degree, the respect and confidence of his neighbors — a man of a large and loving heart, whose efforts and sacrifices for his children were repaid by them with most affectionate veneration. The energy and good sense of his mother exerted a strong influence upon the minds and characters of her children. He was born to the discipline of poverty; but a poverty such as braces and stimulates, not such as crushes and paralyzes. The region in which his boyhood was passed was new and wild, books were not easy to be had, schools were only an occasional privilege, and intercourse with the more settled parts of the country was difficult and rare. But this scarcity of mental food and mental excitement had its advantages, and his training was good, however imperfect his teaching might have been. His labors upon the farm helped to form that vigorous constitution which enabled him to sustain the immense pressure of cares and duties laid upon him in after years. Such books as he could procure were read with the whole heart and the whole mind. The conversation of a household, presided over by a strong-minded father, and a sensible, loving mother, helped to train the faculties of the younger members of the family. Nor were their winter evenings wanting in topics which had a fresher interest than any which books could furnish. There were stirring tales of the revolutionary struggle, and the old French war, in both of which his father had taken a part, with moving traditions of the hardships and perils of border life, and harrowing narratives of Indian captivity, all of which sunk deep into the heart of the impressible boy. The ample page of nature was ever before his eyes, not beautiful or picturesque, but stern, wild, and solitary, covered with a primeval forest, in winter, swept over by tremendous storms, but in summer, putting on a short-lived grace, and in autumn, glowing with an imperial pomp of coloring. In the deep, lonely woods, by the rushing streams, under the frosty stars of winter, the musing boy gathered food for his growing mind. There, to him, the mighty mother unveiled her awful face, and there, we may be sure, that the dauntless child stretched forth his hands and smiled.

We feel a pensive pleasure in calling up the image of this slender, dark-browed, bright-eyed youth, going forth in the morning of life to sow the seed of future years. A loving brother, and a loving and dutiful son, he is cheerful under privation, and patient under restraint. Whatever work he finds to do, whether with the brain or the hand, he does it with all his might. He opens his mind to every ray of knowledge that breaks in upon him. Every step is a progress, and every blow removes an obstacle. Onward, ever onward, he moves; borne "against the wind, against the tide," by an impulse self-derived and self-sustained. He makes friends, awakens interest, inspires hopes. Thus, with these good angels about him, he passes from boyhood to youth, and from youth to early manhood. The school and the college have given him what they had to give; an excellent professional training has been secured; and now, with a vigorous frame, and a spirit patient of labor, with manly self-reliance, and a heart glowing with generous ambition and warm affections, the man, Daniel Webster, steps forth into the arena of life.

From this point his progress follows a natural law of growth, and every advance is justified and explained by what had gone before. For every thing that he gains he has a perfect title to show. He is borne on by no fortunate accidents. The increase of his influence keeps no more than pace with the growth of his mind, and the development of his character. He is diligent in his calling, and faithful to the interests intrusted to his charge. His professional bearing is manly and elevated. He has the confidence of the court, and the ear of the jury, and has fairly earned them both. His business increases, his reputation is extended, and he becomes a marked man. He is not only equal to every occasion, but he always leaves the impression of having power in reserve, and of being capable of still greater efforts. What he does is judicious, and what he says is wise. He is not obliged to retrace his steps or qualify his statements. He blends the dignity and self-command of mature life with the ardor and energy of youth. To such a man, in our country, public life becomes a sort of necessity. A brief service in Congress wins for him the respect and admiration of the leading men of the whole Union, who see, with astonishment, in a young New Hampshire lawyer, the large views of a ripe statesman, and a generous and comprehensive tone of discussion, free alike from party bias and sectional narrowness. A removal to the metropolis of New England brings increase of professional opportunity, and in a few years he stands at the head of the Bar of the whole country. Public life is again thrust upon him, and, at one stride, he moves to the foremost rank of influence and consideration. His prodigious powers of argument and eloquence, freely given to an administration opposed to him in politics, crush a dangerous political heresy, and kindle a deeper national sentiment. The whole land rings with his name and praise, and foreign nations take up and prolong the sound. Every year brings higher trusts, weightier responsibilities, wider influence, until his country reposes in the shadow of his wisdom, and the power that proceeds from his mind and character becomes one of the controlling forces in the movements and relations of the civilized world.

To trace, step by step, the incidents of such a career, would far transcend the limits of a discourse like this, and of all places, it is least needed here. Judging of him by what he was, as well as by what he did, and analyzing the aggregate of his powers, we observe that his life moves in three distinct paths of greatness. He was a great lawyer, a great statesman, and a great writer. The gifts and training, which make a man eminent in any one of these departments, are by no means identical with those which make him eminent in any other. Very few have attained high rank in any two; and the distinction which Mr. Webster reached in all the three is almost without a parallel in history.

He was, from the beginning, more or less occupied with public affairs, and he continued to the last to be a practising lawyer; but, as regards these two spheres of action, his life may be divided into two distinct portions. From his twenty-third to his forty-first year, the practice of the law was his primary occupation and interest, but from the latter period to his death, it was secondary to his labors as a legislator and statesman. Of his eminence in the law — meaning the law as administered in the ordinary tribunals of the country, without reference, for the present, to constitutional questions — there is but one opinion among competent judges. Some may have excelled him in a single faculty or accomplishment, but in the combination of qualities which the law requires, no man of his time was on the whole equal to him. He was a safe counsellor and a powerful advocate; thorough in the preparation of causes and judicious in the management of them; quick, far-seeing, cautious, and bold. His addresses to the jury were simple, manly, and direct; presenting the strong points of the case in a strong way, appealing to the reason and the conscience, and not to passions and prejudices; and never weakened by over-statement. He laid his own mind fairly along-side that of the jury, and won their confidence by his sincere way of dealing with them. He had the wisdom to cease speaking when he had come to an end. His most conspicuous power was his clearness of statement. He threw upon every subject a light like that of the sun at noonday. His mind, by an unerring instinct, separated the important from the unimportant facts in a complicated case, and so presented the former, that he was really making a powerful and persuasive argument, when he seemed to be only telling a plain story in a plain way. The transparency of the stream veiled its depth; and its depth concealed its rapid flow. His legal learning was accurate and perfectly at command, and he had made himself master of some difficult branches of law, such as special pleading and the law of real property, but the memory of some of his contemporaries was more richly stored with cases. From his remarkable powers of generalization, his elementary reading had filled his mind with principles, and he examined the questions that arose, by the light of these principles, and then sought in the books for cases to confirm the views which he had reached by reflection. He never resorted to stratagems and surprises, nor did he let his zeal for his client run away with his self-respect. His judgment was so clear, and his moral sense so strong, that he never could help discriminating between a good cause and a bad one; nor betraying to a close observer when he was arguing against what was his own judgment of his case. His manner was admirable, especially for its repose, an effective quality in an advocate, from the consciousness of strength which it implies. The uniform respect with which he treated the bench should not be omitted, in summing up his merits as a lawyer.

The exclusive practice of the law is not held to be the best preparation for public life. Not only does it invigorate without expanding — not only does it narrow at the same time that it sharpens — but the custom of addressing juries begets a habit of overstatement, which is a great defect in a public speaker, and the mind, that is constantly occupied in looking at one side of a disputed question, is apt to forget that it has two. Great minds triumph over these influences, but it is because they never fail, sooner or later, to overleap the formal barriers of the law. Had Mr. Webster been born in England, and educated to the bar, his powers could never have been confined to Westminster Hall. He would have been taken up and borne into Parliament by an irresistible tide of public opinion. Born where he was, it would have been the greatest of misfortunes, if he had narrowed his mind and given up to his clients the genius that was meant for the whole country and all time. Admirably as he put a case to the jury, or argued it to the court, it was impossible not to feel that in many instances an inferior person would have done it nearly or quite as well; and sometimes the disproportion between the man and the work was so great, that it reminded one of the task given to Michael Angelo, to make a statue of snow.

His advancing reputation, however, soon led him into a class of cases, the peculiar growth of the institutions of his country, and admirably fitted to train a lawyer for public life, because, though legal in their form, they involve great questions of politics and government. The system under which we live is, in many respects, without a precedent. Singularly complicated in its arrangements, embracing a general government of limited and delegated powers, organized by an interfusion of separate sovereignties, all with written constitutions to be interpreted and reconciled, the imperfection of human language and the strength of human passion, leaving a wide margin for warring opinions, it is obvious to any person of political experience, that many grave questions, both of construction and conflicting jurisdiction, must arise, requiring wisdom and authority for their adjustment. Especially must this be the case in a country like ours, of such great extent, with such immense material resources, and inhabited by so enterprising and energetic a people. It was a fortunate, may we not say a providential circumstance, that the growth of the country begun to devolve upon the Supreme Court of the United States the consideration of this class of questions, just at the time when Mr. Webster, in his ripe manhood, was able to give them the benefit of his extraordinary powers of argument and analysis. Previous to the Dartmouth College case, in 1818, not many important constitutional questions had come before the court, and, since that time, the great lawyer, who then broke upon them with so astonishing a blaze of learning and logic, has exerted a commanding influence in shaping that system of constitutional law—almost a supplementary Constitution—which has contributed so much to our happiness and prosperity. Great as is our debt of gratitude to such judges as Marshall and Story, it is hardly less great to such a lawyer as Mr. Webster. None would have been more ready than these eminent magistrates, to acknowledge the assistance they had derived from his masterly arguments.

In the discussion of constitutional questions, the mind of this great man found a most congenial employment. Here, books, cases, and precedents are of comparatively little value. We must ascend to first principles, and be guided by the light of pure reason. Not only is a chain of logical deduction to be fashioned, but its links must first be forged. Geometry itself hardly leads the mind into a region of more abstract and essential truth. In these calm heights of speculation and analysis, the genius of Mr. Webster moved with natural and majestic sweep. Breaking away from precedents and details, and soaring above the flight of eloquence, it saw the forms of truth in the colorless light and tranquil air of reason. When we dream of intelligences higher than man, we imagine their faculties exercised in serene inquisitions like these,—not spurred by ambition—not kindled by passion — roused by no motive but the love of truth, and seeking no reward but the possession of it.

The respect which has been paid to the decisions of the Supreme Court of the United States is one of the signs of hope for the future, which are not to be overlooked in our desponding moods. The visitor in Washington sees a few grave men, in an unpretending room, surrounded by none of the symbols of command. Some one of them, in a quiet voice, reads an opinion in which the conflicting rights of sovereign States are weighed and adjusted, and questions, such as have generally led to exhausting wars, are settled by the light of reason and justice. This judgment goes forth, backed by no armed force, but commended by the moral and intellectual authority of the tribunal which pronounces it. It falls upon the waves of controversy with reconciling, subduing power; and haughty sovereignties, as at the voice of some superior intelligence, put off the mood of conflict and defiance, and yield a graceful obedience to the calm decrees of central justice. There is more cause for national pride in the deference paid to the decisions of this august tribunal, than in all our material triumphs; and so long as our people are thus loyal to reason and submissive to law, it is a weakness to despair.

The Dartmouth College case, which has been already mentioned, may be briefly referred to again, since it forms an important era in Mr. Webster's life. His argument in that case stands out among his other arguments, as his speech in reply to Mr. Hayne, among his other speeches. No better argument has been spoken in the English tongue in the memory of any living man, nor is the child that is born to-day likely to live to hear a better. Its learning is ample, but not ostentatious; its logic irresistible; its eloquence vigorous and lofty. I have often heard my revered and beloved friend, Judge Story, speak with great animation of the effect he then produced upon the court. "For the first hour," said he, "we listened to him with perfect astonishment; for the second hour, with perfect delight; and for the third hour, with perfect conviction." It is not too much to say that he entered the court on that day a comparatively unknown name, and left it with no rival but Pinkney. All the words he spoke on that occasion have not been recorded. When he had exhausted the resources of learning and logic, his mind passed naturally and simply into a strain of feeling not common to the place. Old recollections and early associations came over him, and the vision of his youth rose up. The genius of the institution where he was nurtured seemed standing by his side in weeds of mourning, with a countenance of sorrow. With suffused eyes, and faltering voice, he broke into an unpremeditated strain of emotion, so strong and so deep, that all who heard him were borne along with it. Heart answered to heart as he spoke, and, when he ceased, the silence and tears of the impassive Bench, as well as of the excited audience, were a tribute to the truth and power of the feeling by which he had been inspired.

With his election to Congress, from the city of Boston, in 1822, the great labors and triumphs of his life begin. From that time until his death, with an interval of about two years after leaving President

Tyler's Cabinet, he was constantly in the public service, as Representative, Senator, or Secretary of State. In this period his biography is included in the history of his country. Without pausing to dwell upon details, and looking at his public life as a whole, let us examine its leading features and guiding principles, and inquire upon what grounds he enjoyed our confidence and admiration, while living, and is entitled to our gratitude when dead.

Public men, in popular governments, are divided into two great classes, statesmen and politicians. The difference between them is like the difference between the artist and the mechanic. The statesman starts with original principles, and is propelled by a self-derived impulse. The politician has his course to choose, and puts himself in a position to make the best use of the forces which lie outside of him. The statesman's genius sometimes fails in reaching its proper sphere, from the want of the politician's faculty; and, on the other hand, the politician's intellectual poverty is never fully apprehended till he has contrived to attain an elevation which belongs only to the statesman. The statesman is often called upon to oppose popular opinion, and never is his attitude nobler than when so doing; but the sagacity of the politician is shown in seeing, a little before the rest of the world, how the stream of popular feeling is about to turn, and so throwing himself upon it, as to seem to be guiding it, while he is only propelled by it. A statesman makes the occasion, but the occasion makes the politician.

Mr. Webster was preëminently a statesman. He

rested his claims upon principles; and by these he was ready to stand or fall. In looking at the endowments which he brought to the service of his country, a prominent rank is to be assigned to that deep and penetrating wisdom which gave so safe a direction to his genius. His imagination, his passions, and his sympathies, were all kept in subordination to this sovereign power. He saw things as they are, neither magnified, nor discolored by prejudice or prepossession. He heard all sides, and did not insist that a thing was true, because he wished it to be true, or because it seemed probable to his first inquiry. His post of observation was the central and fixed light of reason, from which all wandering and uncertain elements were at last discerned in their just relations and proportions. The functions of government did not, in his view, lie in the region of speculation or emotion. It was "a contrivance of human wisdom to provide for human wants." The ends of government are, indeed, ever identical, but the means used to attain them are various. The practical statesman must aim, not at the best conceivable, but the best attainable good. Thus, Mr. Webster always recognized and accepted the necessities of his position. He did not hope against hope, nor waste his energies in attempting the impossible. Living under a government, in which universal suffrage is the ultimate propelling force, he received the expressed sense of the people as a fact, and not an hypothesis. Like all men who are long in public life, under popular institutions, he incurred the reproach of inconsistency; a reproach not resting upon any change of principle — for he never changed his principles,—but upon the modification of measures and policy which every enlightened statesman yields to the inevitable march of events and innovations of time.

Nor was he less remarkable for the breadth and comprehensiveness of his views. He knew no North, no South, no East, no West. His great mind and patriotic heart embraced the whole land with all its interests and all its claims. He had nothing of partisan narrowness or sectional exclusiveness. His point of sight was high enough to take in all parts of the country, and his heart was large enough and warm enough to love it all, to cling to it, live for it, or die for it. Nothing is more characteristic of greatness than this capacity of enlarged and generous affections. No public man ever earned more fully the title of a national, an American statesman. No heart ever beat with a higher national spirit than his. The honor of his country was as dear to him as the faces of his children. Where that was in question, his great powers blazed forth like a flame of fire in its defence. Never were his words more weighty, his logic more irresistible, his eloquence more lofty—never did his mind move with more majestic and victorious flight,—than when vindicating the rights of his country, or shielding her from unjust aspersions.

It is a hasty and mistaken judgment to gauge the merits of a statesman, under popular institutions, by the results which he brings about and the measures which he carries through. His opportunities in this respect will depend, generally, upon the fact whether he happens to be in the majority or the minority.

How much would be taken from the greatness of one of the greatest of statesmen, Mr. Fox, if this test were applied to him. The merits of a statesman are to be measured by the good which he does, by the evil which he prevents, by the sentiments he breathes into the public heart, and the principles he diffuses through the public mind. Mr. Webster did not belong to that great political party which, under ordinary circumstances, and when no exceptional elements have been thrown in, have been able to command a majority in the whole nation, and upon which the responsibility of governing the country, has been consequently thrown. Thus, for the larger part of his public life, he was in the minority. But a minority is as important an element, in carrying on a representative government, as a majority; and he never transcended its legitimate functions. His opposition was open, manly, and conscientious; never factious, never importunate. He stated fairly the arguments to which he replied. He did not stoop to personality, or resort to the low and cheap trick of impugning the motives or characters of his opponents. He has therefore fairly earned the respect which the democratic party, to their honor be it spoken, have shown to his memory. He was a party man, to this extent — he believed that under a popular government, it was expedient that men of substantially the same way of thinking in politics should act together, in order to accomplish any general good, but he never gave up to his party what was meant for his country. When the turn of the tide threw upon him the initiative of measures, no man ever showed a wiser spirit of legislation or a more just and enlightened policy in statesmanship. He combined what Bacon calls the logical with the mathematical part of the mind. He could judge well of the mode of attaining any end, and estimate, at the same time, the true value of the end itself. His powers were by no means limited to attack and defence, but he had the organizing and constructing mind, which shapes and fits a course of policy to the wants and temper of a great people.

His influence, as a public man, extends over the last forty years, and, during that period, what is there that does not bear his impress? Go where we will, upon land or sea — from agriculture to commerce, and from commerce to manufactures — turn to domestic industry, to foreign relations, to law, education, and religion, — everywhere, we meet the image and superscription of this imperial mind. The Ashburton treaty may stand as a monument of the good he did. His speech in reply to Mr. Hayne may be cited as a proof of the evil he prevented; and, for this reason, while its whole effect can never be measured, its importance can hardly be overstated. Probably no discourse ever spoken by man had a wider, more permanent, and more beneficial influence. Not only did it completely overthrow a most dangerous attack on the Constitution, but it made it impossible for the same attack ever to be renewed. From that day forward the specious front of nullification was branded with treason. If we estimate the claims of a public man by his influence upon the national heart, and his contributions to a high-toned national sentiment, who shall stand by the side of Mr. Webster?

Where is the theory of constitutional liberty better expounded, and the rules and conditions of national well-being and well-doing better laid down, than in his speeches and writings? What books should we so soon put into the hands of an intelligent foreigner, who desired to learn the great doctrines of government and administration on which the power and progress of our country repose, and to measure the intellectual stature of a finished American man?

The relation which he held to the politics of the country was the natural result of a mind and temperament like his. A wise patriot, who understands the wants of his time, will throw himself into the scale which most needs the weight of his influence, and choose the side which is best for his country and not for himself. Hence, it may be his duty to espouse defeat and cleave to disappointment. In weighing the two elements of law and liberty, as they are mingled in our country, he felt that danger was rather to be apprehended from the preponderance of license than of authority; that men were attracted to liberty by the powerful instincts of the blood and heart, but to law by the colder and fainter suggestions of the reason. Hence, he was a conservative at home, and gave his influence to the party of permanence rather than progression. But in Europe it was different. There he saw that there were abuses to be reformed and burdens to be removed; that the principle of progress was to be encouraged, and that larger infusions of liberty should be poured into the exhausted frames of decayed states. Hence, his sympathies were always on the side of the struggling and the suffering; and, through his powerful voice, the public opinion of America made itself heard and respected in Europe. It is a fact worthy of being stated in this connection, that at the moment when a tempest of obloquy was beating upon him, from his supposed hostility to the cause of freedom here, a very able writer of the Catholic faith, in a striking and, in many respects, admirable essay upon his writings and public life, came reluctantly and respectfully to the conclusion that Mr. Webster had forfeited all claim to the support of Catholic voters, from the countenance he had given to the revolutionary spirit of Europe. Such are ever the judgments of fragmentary men upon a universal man.

His strong sense of the value of the Union, and the force and frequency with which he discoursed upon this theme, are to be explained by the same traits of mind and character. He believed that we were more in danger of diffusion than consolidation. He felt that all the primal instincts of patriotism — all the chords of the heart — bound men to their own State, and not to the common Country; and that with the territorial increase of that country, it became more and more difficult for the central heart to propel to the extremities the life-blood of that invigorating national sentiment, without which a state is but a political corporation without a soul. He knew too, that the name of a Union might exist without the substance, and that a Union for mutual annoyance and defiance, and not for mutual aid and support, which kept the word of promise to the ear and broke it to the hope, was hardly worth the having. Hence, he labored earnestly and perseveringly to inculcate a love of the Union, and to present the whole country as an object to be cherished, honored and valued, because he felt that on that side our affections needed to be quickened and strengthened.

As was to be expected, so powerful a man could not pass through life without encountering strong opposition. All his previous experiences, however, were inconsiderable in comparison with the storm of denunciation which he drew down upon himself by his course on what are commonly called the compromise measures, and, especially, his speech on that occasion. It was natural that men, whose fervid sympathies are wedded to a single idea, should have felt aggrieved by the stand he then took; and if decency and decorum had governed their expressions, neither he nor his friends could have had any right to complain. But, in many cases, the attacks were so foul and ferocious that they lost all claim to be treated as moral judgments, and sunk to the level of the lowest and coarsest effusions of malice and hatred. It is a good rule in politics, as elsewhere, to give men credit for the motives they profess to be actuated by, and to accept their own exposition of their opinions as true. Let us apply these rules to his course at that time. He had opposed the admission of Texas, and predicted the train of evils which would come with it. He had warned the North of the perilous questions with which that measure was fraught. But his prophetic voice was unheeded. Between zeal on one side, and apathy on the other, Texas came in. Then war with Mexico followed, ending in conquest, and leaving the whole of that unhappy country at our mercy. Mr. Webster opposed the dismemberment of Mexico, provided for in the treaty of peace, on the ground that no sooner should we have the immense territory which we proposed to take, than the question whether slavery should exist there, would agitate the country. But again the warning voice of his wisdom was unheeded, and the storm, which he had predicted, gathered in the heavens. The questions against which he had forewarned his countrymen now clamored for settlement, and would not be put by. They required for their adjustment the most of reason and the least of passion, and they were met in a mood which combined the most of passion and the least of reason. The North and the South met in "angry parle," and the air was darkened with their strife. Mr. Webster's prophetic spirit was heavy within him. He felt that a crisis had arrived in the history of his country, and that the lot of a solemn duty and a stern self-sacrifice had fallen upon him. As he himself said, "he had made up his mind to embark alone on what he was aware would prove a stormy sea, because, in that case, should disaster ensue, there would be but one life lost." In this mood of calm and high resolve he went forward to meet the portentous issue.

It is not to be expected that a speech, made under such circumstances, going over so wide a range of exciting topics, should, in every part, command the immediate and entire assent even of those who would admit its truth and seasonableness as a whole. It is also doubtless true, that there are single expressions in it which, when torn from their context, and set by the side of passages from former speeches, dealt with in like manner, will not be found absolutely identical. But the speech of such a man, at such a crisis, is not to be dissected and criticized like a rhetorical exercise. It should be judged as a whole, and read by the light of the occasion which gave it birth.

The judgments which Mr. Webster's course has called forth, were widely diverse. By those who hold extreme views, he was charged with expressing sentiments which he did not believe to be true. It was "a bid for the Presidency," and his conscience was the price he offered. It is a mere waste of words to argue with men of this class. Fanaticism darkens the mind and hardens the heart, and where there is neither common sense nor common charity, the first step in a process of reasoning cannot be taken. Others maintained that he was mistaken in point of fact, that he took counsel of his fears and not of his wisdom, and, that through him, the opportunity was lost of putting down the South in an open struggle for influence and power. But, in the first place, it is not probable that a man, who, upon subordinate questions, had shown so much political wisdom and forecast, should have been mistaken upon a point of such transcendent importance, to which his attention had been so long and so earnestly directed; and, in the second place, the testimony of nearly all men, whose evidence would be received with respect upon any similar subject, fully sustains Mr. Webster in the views he then took of the state of the country, and is equally strong as to the value of the services he rendered. In such an issue, the testimony of retired persons, living among books and their own thoughts, is not entitled to any great value, because they can have no adequate notion of the duties, responsibilities, or difficulties of governing a great State, and what need there is of patience and denunciation in those who are called to this highest of human functions. A statesman has the right to be tried by his peers.

It is curious to observe how hatred, whether personal or political, when it enters into the mind, disturbs its functions, as a piece of iron, in the binnacle of a ship, misleads the compass. Many, who have found it so hard to forgive Mr. Webster for his independence in opposing them, would admit the importance of having a class of public men, who will lead the people and not be led by them, and that a great man is never so great, as when withstanding their dangerous wishes, and calmly braving their anger. Their eyes will sparkle when they speak of the neutral countenance of Washington, undismayed by jacobin clamor, and of the sublime self-devotion of Jay. It is strange that they cannot, or will not, for a moment, look at Mr. Webster's position from a point of view opposite to their own, admit that he may have been in the right, and see him clad in the beauty of self-sacrifice. It is to be feared that this form of virtue is growing more and more rare, as it is more and more needed. The story of Curtius leaping into a gulf in the Roman Forum, in order to save his country, is but the legendary form in which a perpetual truth is clothed. In the path of time there are always chasms of error which only a great self-immolating victim can close. The glory has departed from the land in which that self-devoting stock has died out.

Mr. Webster was an ambitious man. He desired the highest office in the gift of the people. But on this subject, as on all others, there was no concealment in his nature. And ambition is not a weakness, unless it be disproportioned to the capacity. To have more ambition than ability is to be at once weak and unhappy. With him it was a noble passion, because it rested upon noble powers. He was a man cast in a heroic mould. His thoughts, his wishes, his passions, his aspirations, were all on a grander scale than those of other men. Unexercised capacity is always a source of rusting discontent. The height to which men may rise is in proportion to the upward force of their genius, and they will never be calm till they have attained their predestined elevation. Lord Bacon says, "as in nature things move violently *to* their place, and calmly *in* their place, so virtue in ambition is violent, in authority, settled and calm." Mr. Webster had a giant's brain and a giant's heart, and he wanted a giant's work. He found repose in those strong conflicts and great duties, which crush the weak and madden the sensitive. He thought that, if he were elevated to the highest place, he should so administer the government as to make the country honored abroad, and great and happy at home. He thought, too, that he could do something to make us more truly one people. This, above every thing else, was his ambition. And we, who knew him better than others, felt that it was a prophetic ambition, and we honored and trusted him accordingly.

As a writer, and as a public speaker, upon the great interests of his country, Mr. Webster stands before us, and will stand before those who come after us, as the leading spirit of his time. Sometimes, indeed, his discussions may have been too grave to be entirely effective, at the moment of their delivery, but all of them are quarries of political wisdom; for while others have solved only the particular problem before them, he has given the rule that reaches all of the same class. As a general remark, his speeches are a striking combination of immediate effectiveness and enduring worth. He never, indeed, goes out of his way for philosophical observations, nor lingers long in the tempting regions of speculation, but his mind, while he advances straight to his main object, drops from its abundant stores those words of wisdom which will keep through all time a vital and germinating power. His logic is vigorous and compact, but there is no difficulty in following his argument, because his reasoning is as clear as it is strong. The leading impression he leaves upon the mind, is that of irresistible weight. We are conscious of a propelling power, before which every thing gives way or goes down. The hand of a giant is upon us, and we feel that it is in vain to struggle. The eloquence of Burke, with whom he is always most fitly compared, is like a broad river, winding through a cultivated landscape; that of Mr. Webster, is like a clear mountain stream, compressed between walls of rock.

But his claims as a writer do not rest exclusively upon his political speeches. His occasional discourses, and his diplomatic writings, would alone make a great reputation. His occasional discourses rise above the rest of their class, as the Bunker Hill Monument soars above the objects around it. His Plymouth oration, especially, is a production which all, who have followed in the same path, must ever look upon with admiration, and despair. It was the beginning of a new era in that department of literature. It was the first and greatest of its class; and has naturally fixed a standard of excellence which has been felt in the efforts of all who have come after him. Its merits of style and treatment are of the highest order, and it is marked throughout by that dignity of sentiment and that elevating and stirring tone of moral feeling which lift the mind into regions higher than can be reached by eloquence alone.

His diplomatic writings claim unqualified praise. Such discussions require a cautious as well as firm hand; for a single rash expression, falling upon an explosive state of mind, may shatter to pieces the most hopeful negotiation. Mr. Webster combines great force of statement with perfect decorum of manner. It is the iron hand, but the silken glove. He neither claims nor yields a single inch beyond the right. His attitude is neither aggressive nor distrustful. He is strong in himself, and strong in his position. His style is noble, dignified, and transparent. It is the "large utterance" of a great people. I know of no modern compositions which, in form and substance, embody so much of what we understand by the epithet, Roman. Such, indeed, we may imagine the state papers of the Roman Senate to have been, in the best days of the Republic.

His arguments, speeches, occasional discourses, and diplomatic writings, have all a marked family likeness. They are all characterized by strength and simplicity. He never goes out of his way to make a point or drag in an illustration. His ornaments, sparingly introduced, are of that pure gold, which defies the sharpest test of criticism. He had more of imagination, properly so called, than fancy, and his images are more grand than picturesque. He writes like a man who is thinking of his subject, and not of his style, and thus wastes no time upon the mere garb of his thoughts. His mind was so full, that epithet and illustration grew with his words, like flowers on the stalk. It is a striking fact, that a man who has had so great an influence over the mind of America, should have been so free from our national defects; our love of exaggeration, and our excessive use of figurative language. His style is Doric, not Corinthian. His sentences are like shafts hewn from the granite of his own hills — simple, massive, and strong. We may apply to him what Quinctilian says of Cicero, that a relish for his writings is itself a mark of good taste. He is always plain; sometimes even homely and unfinished. But a great writer may be, and indeed must be, homely and unfinished at times. Dealing with great subjects, he must vary his manner. Some things he will put in the foreground, and some in the background; some in light, and some in shadow. He will not hesitate, therefore, to say plain things in a plain way. When the glow and impulse of his genius are upon him, he will not stop to adjust every fold in his mantle. His writings will leave upon the mind an effect, like that of the natural landscape upon the eye, where nothing is trim and formal, but where all the sweeps and swells, though rarely conforming to an ideal line of beauty, blend together in a general impression of grace, fertility, and power.

His knowledge of law, politics, and government was profound, various, and exact; but a man of learning, in the sense in which this word is commonly used, he could not be called. His life had been too busy to leave much time for prolonged scientific or literary research; nor had he that passionate love of books which made him content to pass all his leisure hours in his library. He had read much, but not many books. He was a better Latin scholar than the average of our educated men, and he read the Roman authors, to the last, with discriminating relish. A mind like his was naturally drawn to the grand and stately march of Roman genius. With the best English writers he was entirely familiar, and he took great pleasure in reading them, and discussing their merits.

To science, as recorded in books, he had given little time, but he had the faculties and organization which would easily have made him a man of science. He had the senses of an Indian hunter. Of the knowledge that is gathered by observation — as of the names and properties of plants, the song and plumage of birds, and the forms and growth of trees — he had much more than most men of his class. His eye was as accurate as his mind was discriminating. Never was his conversation more interesting than when speaking of natural objects and natural phenomena.

His words had the freshness of morning, and seemed to bring with them the breezes of the hills and the fragrance of spring.

Mr. Webster, both as a writer and a speaker, was unequal, and from the nature of his mind and temperament, it could not be otherwise. He was not of an excitable organization, and felt no nervous anxiety lest he should fall below the standard of expectation raised by previous efforts. Hence, he was swayed by the mood, mental or physical, in which each occasion found him. He required a great subject, or a great antagonist, to call forth all his slumbering power. At times, he looked and spoke almost like a superhuman creature; at others, he seemed but the faint reflex of himself. His words fell slowly and heavily from his lips, as if each cost him a distinct effort. The influence, therefore, which he had over popular assemblies, was partly owing to his great weight of character.

He had strong out-of-door tastes, and they contributed to the health of his body and mind. He was a keen sportsman, and a lover of the mountains and the sea. His heart warmed to a fine tree as to the face of a friend. He had that fondness for agriculture and rural pursuits so common among statesmen. Herein the grand scale of the whole man gave direction and character to his tastes. He did not care for minute finish and completeness on a limited scale. He had no love for trim gardens and formal pleasure grounds. His wishes clasped the whole landscape. He liked to see broad fields of clover, with the morning dew upon them, yellow waves of grain, heaving and rolling in the sun, and great cattle lying down in the shade of great trees. He liked to hear the whetting of the mower's scythe, the loud beat of the thresher's flail, and the heavy groan of loaded wagons. The smell of the new-mown hay, and of the freshly-turned furrows in spring, was cordial to his spirit. He took especial pleasure in all forms of animal life, and his heart was glad when his cattle lifted up their large-eyed, contemplative faces, and recognized their lord by a look.

His mental powers were commended by a remarkable personal appearance. He was probably the grandest looking man of his time. Wherever he went, men turned to gaze at him; and he could not enter a room without having every eye fastened upon him. His face was very striking, both in form and color. His brow was to common brows, what the great dome of St. Peters is to the smaller cupolas at its side. The eyebrow, the eye, and the dark and deep socket in which it glowed, were full of power; but the great expression of his face lay in the mouth. This was the most speaking and flexible of features, moulded by every mood of feeling, from iron severity to the most captivating sweetness. His countenance changed from sternness to softness with magical rapidity. His smile was beaming, warming, fascinating; lighting up his whole face like a sudden sunrise. His voice was rich, deep, and strong; filling the largest space without effort, capable of most startling and impressive tones, and, when under excitement, rising and swelling into a volume of sound, like the roar of a tempest. His action was simple and dignified; and in his animated moods, highly expressive. Those of us who recall his presence as he stood up here to speak, in the pride and strength of his manhood, have formed from his words, looks, tones, and action, an ideal standard of physical and intellectual power, which we never expect to see approached, but by which we unconsciously try, not only the greatness we meet, but that of which we read.

He was a man more known and admired than understood. His great qualities were conspicuous from afar; but that part of his nature, which he shared with other men, was apprehended by comparatively few. His manners did not always do him justice. For many years of his life, great burdens rested upon him, and, at times, his cares and thoughts settled down darkly upon his spirit, and he was then a man of an awful presence. He required to be loved before he could be known. He, indeed, grappled his friends to him with hooks of steel, but he did not always conciliate those who were not his friends. He had a lofty spirit, which could not stoop or dissemble. He could neither affect what he did not feel, nor desire to conceal what he did. His wishes clung with tenacious hold to every thing they grasped, and from those who stood, or seemed to stand, in his way, his countenance was averted. Some, who were not unwilling to become his friends, were changed by his manner into foes. He was social in his nature, but not facile. He was seen to the best advantage among a few old and tried friends, especially in his own home. Then his spirits rose, his countenance expanded, and he looked and moved like a school-boy on a holiday. Conscious that no unfriendly ear was listening to him, his conversation became easy, playful, and natural. His memory was richly stored with characteristic anecdotes, and with amusing reminiscences of his own early life, and of the men who were conspicuous when he was young, all of which he narrated with an admirable mixture of dignity and grace. Those who saw him in these hours of social ease, with his armor off, and the current of his thoughts turning, gently and gracefully, to chance topics and familiar themes, could hardly believe that he was the same man who was so reserved and austere in public.

But it may be asked, had this great man no faults? Surely he had. No man liveth, and sinneth not. There were veins of human imperfection running through his large heart and large brain. But neither men, nor the works of men, should be judged by their defects. Like all eminent persons he fell upon evil tongues; but those who best knew his private life, most honored, venerated, and loved him.

He was a man of strong religious feeling. For theological speculations he had little taste, but he had reflected deeply on the relations between God and the human soul, and his heart was penetrated with a devotional spirit. He had been, from his youth upwards, a diligent student of the Scriptures, and few men, whether clergymen or laymen, were more familiar with their teachings and their language. He had a great reverence for the very words of the Bible, and never used them in any light or trivial connection. He never avoided the subjects of life, death, and immortality, and when he spoke of them, it was with unusual depth of feeling and impressiveness of manner.

Within the last few months of his life, his thoughts and speech were often turned upon such themes. He felt that he was an old man, and that it became him to set his house in order. On the eighteenth day of January last, he had completed the threescore and ten years, which are man's allotted portion, and yet his eye was not dim, nor his natural force much abated. But he grew weaker with the approach of summer, and his looks and voice, when he last addressed us from this place, a few months ago, forced upon us the mournful reflection that this great light must soon sink below the horizon. But yet, when the news came that the hand of death was upon him, it startled us like a sudden blow, for he was become so important to us, that we could not look steadily at the thought of losing him. You remember what a sorrow it was that settled down upon our city. The common business of life dragged heavily with us in those days. There was but one expression on the faces of men, and but one question on their lips. We listened to the tidings which came up, hour after hour, from his distant chamber, as men upon the shore in a night of storm, listen to the minute-guns of a sinking ship, freighted with the treasures of their hearts. The grief of the people was eager for the minutest details of his closing hours, and he died with his country around his bed. Of the beauty and grandeur of that death I need not speak to you, for it is fixed in your memories and deep in your hearts. It fell upon the whole land like a voice from Heaven. He died calmly, simply, and bravely. He was neither weary of life, nor afraid of death. He died like a husband, a father, a friend, a Christian, and a man; with thoughtful tenderness for all around him, and a trembling faith in the mercy of God. He was not tried by long and hopeless suffering; nor were his friends saddened by seeing the spirit darkened before it was released. His mind, like a setting sun, seemed largest at the closing hour. Such a death narrows the dark valley to a span. Such is a midsummer's day at the poles, where sunset melts into sunrise, and the last ray of evening is caught up and appears once more as the first beam of the new morning.

I should not feel that my duty had been wholly discharged, did I not speak of the touching simplicity and solemnity of his funeral. In his will, made a few days before his death, he says, "I wish to be buried without the least show or ostentation, but in a manner respectful to my neighbors, whose kindness has contributed so much to the happiness of me and mine, and for whose prosperity I offer sincere prayers to God." His wishes were faithfully observed, and, in the arrangements for his funeral, there was no recognition of worldly distinction or official rank. He was buried simply as the head of a household, after the manner of New England. But the immense crowds which were there, drawn from all parts of the land by their own veneration and love, formed an element of impressiveness far above all civic pageantry or military honors. Who, that was there present, will ever forget the scene on which fell the rich light of that soft autumnal day. There was the landscape, so stamped with his image and identified with his presence. There were the trees he had planted, the fields over which he had delighted to walk, and the ocean whose waves were music to his ear. There was the house, with its hospitable door; but the stately form of its master did not stand there, with outstretched hand, and smile of welcome. That smile had vanished forever from the earth, and the hand and form were silent, cold, and motionless. The dignity of life had given place to the dignity of death. No narrow chamber held that illustrious dust; no coffin concealed that majestic frame. In the open air, clad as when alive, he lay extended in seeming sleep; with no touch of disfeature upon his brow; as noble an image of reposing strength as ever was seen upon earth. Around him was the landscape that he had loved, and above him was nothing but the dome of the covering heavens. The sunshine fell upon the dead man's face, and the breeze blew over it. A lover of nature, he seemed to be gathered into her maternal arms, and to lie like a child upon a mother's lap. We felt, as we looked upon him, that death had never stricken down, at one blow, a greater sum of life. And whose heart did not swell, when, from the honored and distinguished men there gathered together from far and near, six plain Marshfield farmers were called forth to carry the head of their neighbor to the grave! Slowly and sadly the vast multitude followed, in mourning silence, and he was laid down to rest among dear and kindred dust. There, among the scenes that he loved in life, he sleeps well. He has left his name and memory to dwell forever upon those hills and valleys, to breathe a more spiritual tone into the winds that blow over his grave, to touch with finer light the line of the breaking wave, to throw a more solemn beauty upon the hues of autumn and the shadows of twilight.

But though his mortal form is there, his spirit is here. His words are written in living light along these walls. May that spirit rest upon us and our children! May those words live in our hearts, and the hearts of those who come after us! May we honor his memory, and show our gratitude for his life, by taking heed to his counsels, and walking in the way on which the light of his wisdom shines!

www.ingramcontent.com/pod-product-compliance
Lightning Source LLC
LaVergne TN
LVHW010225110826
845151LV00004B/1188

* 9 7 8 1 4 2 5 5 2 6 0 3 0 *